SOMACULTURAL LIBERATION

ROGER KUHN, PHD

SOMACULTURAL LIBERATION

An Indigenous, Two-Spirit Somatic Guide to Integrating Cultural Experiences Toward Freedom

North Atlantic Books
Huichin, unceded Ohlone land
Berkeley, California

Published by
North Atlantic Books
Huichin, unceded Ohlone land
Berkeley, California

Cover design by Aashim Raj
Book design by Happenstance Type-O-Rama

Printed in the United States of America

Somacultural Liberation: An Indigenous, Two-Spirit Somatic Guide to Integrating Cultural Experiences Toward Freedom is sponsored and published by North Atlantic Books, an educational nonprofit based in the unceded Ohlone land Huichin (Berkeley, CA) that collaborates with partners to develop cross-cultural perspectives; nurture holistic views of art, science, the humanities, and healing; and seed personal and global transformation by publishing work on the relationship of body, spirit, and nature.

North Atlantic Books' publications are distributed to the US trade and internationally by Penguin Random House Publisher Services. For further information, visit our website at www.northatlanticbooks.com.

Disclaimer: This book is not a substitute for any psychotherapy you may need. Although I do believe there are tools you can utilize throughout this book that may benefit you in your healing journey, if you need them, I encourage you to take what you may learn about yourself while reading this book to a psychotherapist who can help you sort through any joys, pains, or liberations this book may bring about. In my work as a psychotherapist and educator, I help people examine and connect to the intersections of their identity so they can understand how culture shapes and informs their bodily experiences. I believe that once we begin to understand ourselves from this somacultural lens, we can learn to better navigate the complex systems we interact with in our lived experiences.

Library of Congress Cataloging-in-Publication Data
Names: Kuhn, Roger, author.
Title: Somacultural liberation : an indigenous, two-spirit somatic guide to integrating cultural experiences towards freedom / Roger Kuhn.
Description: Berkeley, CA : North Atlantic Books, [2024] | Includes bibliographical references.
Identifiers: LCCN 2023020538 (print) | LCCN 2023020539 (ebook) | ISBN 9781623178826 (trade paperback) | ISBN 9781623178833 (ebook)
Subjects: LCSH: Movement therapy. | Cultural psychiatry. | Two-spirit people—Psychology.
Classification: LCC RC489.M66 K84 2024 (print) | LCC RC489.M66 (ebook) | DDC 616.89/165—dc23/eng/20230905
LC record available at https://lccn.loc.gov/2023020538
LC ebook record available at https://lccn.loc.gov/2023020539

1 2 3 4 5 6 7 8 9 KPC 28 27 26 25 24

This book includes recycled material and material from well-managed forests. North Atlantic Books is committed to the protection of our environment. We print on recycled paper whenever possible and partner with printers who strive to use environmentally responsible practices.

To those who paved the way,
those keeping the path clear,
and those who will build a brighter future.
Mvto, thank you.

CONTENTS

ACKNOWLEDGMENTS

This book was written on occupied Indigenous territories in the lands now known as the United States of America, Mexico, and Costa Rica. I send my gratitude to the Cahuilla, Kumeyaay, Ohlone, and Pomo people whose territories exist in the lands in which portions of this book were written, in what is now known as the state of California, and in the cities now known as Palm Springs, San Diego, San Francisco, and Guerneville. Portions of this book were written in Puerto Jimenez, Costa Rica (Buglé and Ngäbé territory), and Mexico City, Mexico (Mexihcah territory). Finally, portions of this book were also written on the reservation of the Poarch Band of Creek Indians (the homelands of my maternal ancestors) surrounded by what is now known as Alabama. I acknowledge the land as an integral entry point into any decolonial and liberation framework.

I want to thank my mother, Joyce Kuhn, my sisters, Tammy King, Diva Kuhn, and Misty Priest, my nieces and nephews, and my larger extended family for being beacons of support through my entire life's journey. I love you all; you mean the world to me. To my friends who I bounced ideas off of and who shared my pains and frustrations about the writing process, your generosity and support are indescribable. Special thanks to Janet Forward, Lori Bohner, Sherri Taylor, Abel Gomez, Adam Bee, Shani Evans, and James Erickson; I am beyond thankful for your friendship. You all make me feel so incredibly loved. To my professional colleagues Doug Braun-Harvey, Roz Dischiavo, Lucy Fielding, Anne Mauro, Bianca Laureano, and Serina Hazelwood Payan, I appreciate all the support you have gifted me. You are all more than colleagues; you too are friends! Also a shout-out to all the musicians who provided the soundtrack I listened to while writing this book. Special mention to the band Lucius, who I listened to the most while writing. Finally, to my best friend, husband, and partner in life, Sean Kreiger; you inspire everything that I do. Sean, you make life more rich, more deep, more profound, and full of an unconditional love I had only dreamed about before we met many moons ago on a cold November night. I love you more than words would ever be able to describe.

My work is inspired and informed by the many artists, poets, writers, and scholars who identify as Two-Spirit and/or advocate for the equity and inclusion of Two-Spirit people. Additionally, the greatest inspiration for my work is the Two-Spirit and Native American/First Nations community. Thank you to my ancestors and elders who persevered through adversity so that I would have a chance to excel in this colonized world. Thank you also to the Two-Spirit ancestors, elders, allies, and accomplices who have fought tirelessly for equity and inclusion; it is upon your shoulders I gently lean.

This book could be written about any number of topics because somacultural liberation is applicable to all ideas and perspectives that do not seek to harm others. One way that I will be writing about and exploring the idea of somacultural liberation is through the lens of Two-Spirit people as well as Indigenous knowledge, epistemologies, and sexuality. I hope others recognize the value of somacultural liberatory ideology and apply it to all kinds of issues, perspectives, and ways of thinking, feeling, and experiencing a life well-lived in a body well-loved.

INTRODUCTION

> I transcend illusion, I'm a pilgrim lost at sea. Somatic attunement I can feel my own body. A fork in the road now, intuition will guide me. My breath, my resilience is the key. My breath, my resilience sets me free.
>
> —ROGER KUHN, PHD, "Before I Rise"

This is a book about connection. Connection with our body. Connection with our culture. Most importantly, connection with the totality of our authentic self (or as much of our authentic self as we are able to feel into). For a period in my early life, I felt disconnected from my body and from my culture, which created a disconnection from my authentic self. I did not fully understand what an authentic self was. I had heard various teachers, spiritual leaders, friends, and therapists I worked with use the term *authentic self* on varying occasions, though I'd never heard anyone explain what the phrase meant. Only recently did I learn a definition that deeply resonated with me. *Authenticity is the intersection of truth and trust* (Oyeneyin, 2022). Please keep this definition in mind whenever you come across the word *authentic* or *authenticity* in this text (and perhaps going forward in your life). Authenticity elicits feelings of anxiety and excitement, two emotions that our bodies experience in very similar ways.

The idea of an authentic-self excited me because it led me to believe that liberation was possible. The idea also made me anxious that I would have to confront and ultimately reveal parts of my identity that I was not ready to fully embrace. Those parts of myself that I was nervous to investigate included my sexuality, my spiritual beliefs, and the complexity of my gender and racial identities. Later on we will discuss *positionality* and *epistemology*, big words that stand for relatively simple ideas: who you are (positionality) and how you know what you know (epistemology).

My hope for all of you engaging with this book is that by the time you have read the final words, you will have a better understanding of how your cultural experiences have affected who you are (positionality) and what you know (epistemology). It is my core belief across all of my disciplines that in order to fully understand our lived experience, we must include an examination of how culture impacts our bodies. I consider my work *somacultural*. This is a phrase I use to highlight my interest in the body (soma) and its relation to culture, which helps shape, challenge, and ultimately influence our experiences. I believe it is valid to question and understand the role of culture in our bodily experiences, and when we can understand this impact better, we can all take another step toward our personal and collective liberation. I am also not the first person to explore culture and body; rather, this is an epistemological inquiry that has been explored across the world for many lifetimes.

Somacultural liberation is a practice-based ideology and is not a replacement for any religious, spiritual, cultural, or mental health practice you currently have in your life. Rather, I invite you to think of somacultural liberation as something you can add to the many practices you may have already incorporated. Although I believe a somacultural framework is an evolving practice over time, it does not need to be a daily practice. It may be a practice you check in with once a month or once a year. Things change in our lives all the time. Seasonal shifts may impact us, or political elections. How do these natural and people-created events impact the experience that we have in the world, which includes the way that we respond in our body? Somacultural liberation also recognizes the varying aspects of positionality, privilege, and power that we engage with on personal and systemic levels. I call the influence of positionality, privilege, and power the *Triple Ps*. I believe when we understand who we are, we can understand and examine the varying privileges we may (or may not) hold, and how all of this relates to power—lived, experienced, and challenged.

Somacultural liberation is a somatic, intellectual, emotional, and existential modality. The *somatic* invites inquiry into proprioceptive and interoceptive awareness, recognizing the way our body moves through spaces externally (proprioception) and internally (interoception) and how our body is shaped by our cultural experiences. The *intellectual* ponders how we think about culture and the stories we have attached to our collective and personal lives. The *emotional* welcomes how we feel about our cultural experiences and the narratives that drive our human experience. Finally, the *existential*, what I also call the spiritual, evokes a sense of wonder wherein we contemplate the questions that remain. Moving through these four spaces will feel familiar to some readers as a process of engagement with the medicine wheel. The *medicine wheel* is an Indigenous healing modality that uses direction, seasons, elements, and human experience to bring us closer to balance. Creation and original application of the medicine wheel is attributed to Native peoples of the North American plains regions and it is now used by many tribal communities (reservation, rural, and urban) across the lands we now refer to as the United States and Canada. The medicine wheel has been appropriated by many non-Native practitioners who have not given credit to the Native communities who created this powerful modality of understanding the totality of the human experience. I give full credit and credence to the Native ancestors who inspired my usage of the medicine wheel in somacultural liberation.

Somacultural liberation is not about *coming out*, a phrase associated with revealing parts of ourselves we have kept hidden from others (and sometimes ourselves); rather, the practice is about returning to ourselves, who we always were. Somacultural liberation is inspired by the Anishinaabeg word *biskaabiiyang*, which when translated into English means "returning to ourselves." Anishinaabe author and creator of the term *Indigenous futurism*, Grace Dillon (2012) defines biskaabiiyang as "discovering how personally one is affected by colonization, discarding the emotional and psychological baggage carried from its impact, and recovering ancestral traditions" (p. 10). Returning to who we were before we were told how to act, dress, speak, believe, worship, hurt, harm, hate. Somacultural liberation is one path to bring us closer, return us to who we truly are: bold, beautiful, bright, balanced creatures of love.

I aspire to achieve transparency in my writing. I believe the best way for me to explain the idea and theory behind somacultural liberation is to invite you into parts of my lived experience as a human being. My own positionality (identity) will be reflected throughout. I invite you to have whatever experience you may have with what I share, and I further invite you to reflect upon any similarities in your own story. How might an experience I am sharing about my life create a reflection about your own life and experience? Because it is a part of my experience, throughout this text I will weave varying historical and contemporary experiences Native American people live with under colonial rule. My inclusion of Native American history is to help you better understand the impact culture has on the body, and since I exist within a mixed-race (Native American and White) body, this is the framework with which I see and understand the world. Though you may not see life through the lens of a mixed-race Poarch Creek Two-Spirit Indigiqueer gay person, can you be open to the possibility that your perspective on life is also based upon your unique somacultural blueprint? My theory behind somacultural liberation is not to advocate for individualism; rather the opposite. My belief is that we must acknowledge the depth and subtly of nuance in cultural understandings, beliefs, and practices to be more closely connected as a community and society.

Throughout this text, you will find exercises and experientials to help you get in touch with your body, your thoughts, your feelings, and the larger questions that are looming in your life. You will learn about using the BOLD ADDRESSING assessment (Hays, 2022; Kuhn, 2021), Window of Tolerance (Siegel, 1999), four spaces (medicine wheel), and Soma-C (Kuhn, 2021). The exercises and experientials will include writing, movement, and mindfulness prompts to help you connect deeper with your somacultural experience and guide you closer to your liberation. *Mvto*! Thank you for joining me on this journey.

KEY TERMINOLOGY

Throughout this book, I use terminology I anticipate many people may not have heard before: *Native/Indigenous*, *Two-Spirit*, *settler colonialism*, *decolonize sexuality*, *unsettle sexuality*, *sexual sovereignty*, and *somacultural*. These concepts are not solely of my creation. Rather, they are continuations of the resiliency, determination, and knowledge Black, Indigenous, and People of Color (BIPOC) communities have experienced through genocide and colonization. I honor and recognize the activists, artists, community organizers, community members, and academics who have created entry points in which decolonization and liberation discourse can thrive. I hope to invoke in the reader an immediate connection to Indigeneity and narratives of decolonization, which have been impacting all bodies on the North American continent since the invasion of the lands known by Native people as Turtle Island. I seek to inform the reader that even though these terms are being used in conjunction with Two-Spirit people, sexual sovereignty and erotic survivance can be applied to all marginalized and oppressed people who continue to heal from what Jolivétte (2016) terms *post traumatic invasion syndrome*, the continued settler and colonial ideology of domination over aspects of a person's or group's identity.

My inclusion of these terms is also inspired by Crenshaw's (1989, 1991) theory of intersectionality. Crenshaw (1989) recognizes the importance of analyzing the intersections of race, class, and ethnicity regarding daily lived experiences because "otherwise-privileged group members create a distorted analysis of racism and sexism because the operative conceptions of race and sex become grounded in experiences that actually represent only a subset of a much more complex phenomenon" (p. 140).

NATIVE/INDIGENOUS I use the terms *Native* and *Indigenous* interchangeably throughout this text. Native/Indigenous are terms that are synonyms for the identities of American Indian, Alaska Native, First Nations, Aboriginal, and Native American. I use these terms purposefully instead of American Indian because the term *Indian* is used by colonial governments and has no real meaning or value to the Indigenous people whose lands the governments of the United States and Canada forcibly took through genocide.

TWO-SPIRIT *Two-Spirit* gained popularity after Dr. Myra Laramee (Fisher River Cree Nation) introduced the term at the third annual International Two-Spirit gathering outside of Winnipeg, Manitoba, in 1990 (Two-Spirited People of Manitoba Inc., 2019). Two-Spirit is often used as an umbrella term for Indigenous people from North America who experience gender and sexual orientation variance. The term also applies to Indigenous people who experience gender and sexual orientation fluidity and who also perform traditional roles in their Native communities. The term Two-Spirit, though sometimes used as an umbrella term for those who may identify as *LGBTQIA+* (lesbian, gay, bisexual, trans, queer/questioning, intersex, asexual) and identify as Native American/American Indian/Indian/First Nations/Aboriginal, is not meant as a replacement for Indigenous languages, which already have a word to describe Two-Spirit people. Two-Spirit was derived from the Northern Algonquin word *niizh manitoag*, meaning "two-spirits," and it is meant to signify the masculine and feminine spirits within one person (Balsam, Huang, Fieland, Simoni, & Walters, 2004, p. 288).

SETTLER COLONIALISM *Settler colonialism* is the projection of Eurocentric culture and values on BIPOC. Settler colonialism includes forced assimilation of language, religion, laws, and ideologies onto non-White bodies. In the context of settler colonialism and Indigenous people, Indigenous men were desexualized, Indigenous women were overtly sexualized, and Indigenous people with gender and sexual orientation variance were ridiculed, abused, and murdered, including by being fed alive to dogs during the Iberian conquest as a form of punishment for sodomy (Trexler, 1997, p. 82).

DECOLONIZE SEXUALITY I define *decolonizing sexuality* as a multitiered process of challenging dominant narratives of sexuality. Decolonizing sexuality is an engaged process that includes the emotional, somatic, spiritual, and sexual experiences that all colonized, oppressed, and marginalized people have a right to explore and claim as part of their sovereignty and lived experiences.

UNSETTLE SEXUALITY *Unsettling sexuality* is an examination and corrective process of disengagement with colonial ideologies, discourse, and rhetoric involving gender, sexual orientation, sexual behavior, heterosexism, heteropatriarchy, racism, and violence. Unsettling sexuality pertains to all peoples living within and under colonial regimes and is most applicable to those who benefit from genocide and indentured servitude.

SEXUAL SOVEREIGNTY *Sexual sovereignty* is a direct challenge to settler colonialism and heterocentric idealism, which fail at understanding how Indigenous communities experience gender and sexuality. Sexual sovereignty is also a claim that Two-Spirit bodies have a right to identify with gender and sexual orientation fluidity and the physical acts of intimacy, pleasure, and sex as an extension of decolonization and a return to Indigenous roles, identities, and practices that existed prior to first contact.

SOMACULTURAL *Somacultural* is an ideology that examines how culture shapes and informs our bodily experiences.

I

THE BODY

This morning I awoke to pangs of anxiety. When I looked at my phone to check the time, it read 4:44 a.m. and I realized I was holding my breath. "Exhale," I told myself. I brought my awareness and intention to the cycle of inhale, pause, exhale, pause. I drew into the sensation of my rib cage expanding, the intrinsic and extrinsic muscles of my rib cage moving in order to aid my respiration. The feeling of anxiety began to present itself in my chest and I felt heaviness around my heart. I needed fresh air. I needed to take a deep breath of fresh air. For the past week I have woken from a deep sleep at approximately 4:30 a.m. every morning. The first thought that leaps into my mind is "write!" I look at my phone, desperate to dissociate by going on social media. "Write!" I hear my voice in my head, demanding that I get out of bed and start writing. I close my eyes but they immediately spring back to life, "write!" I begin to get a yearning sensation; my kidneys have done their function while I was sleeping, and I need to urinate. My feet hit the floor and I immediately notice a tight sensation on the soles of my feet. I know that I've been tensing while I'm sleeping again; must be anxiety; "write!"

The bathroom floor feels cool against my feet, which seems to please my aching plantar tissue. I relieve myself and desire to go back to bed, although I'm not very tired. I look down the short hall to my inviting bed and start to turn toward the warmth of my husband and dogs when I'm suddenly struck by the sound of my voice—"write!" "Write!" Yes, I know that I should begin to write, but where to begin? I sit down in front of my computer and notice my jaw is throbbing. Like I do with my feet, I also clench my jaw when I'm having bouts of anxiety. I know the anxiety is stemming from my need to write this book and be sure I turn in my manuscript on time. I massage my jaw at the temporal mandibular joint and am confronted by my voice again: "write!"

A slight burning sensation develops at the top of my chest, which I know to be anxiety and not acid reflux. It's 4:50 a.m. and I'm having an anxiety attack because I'm thinking that I'm not thinking enough. I try to deepen my breath, close my eyes, and clear my mind. "Write!" I hear my voice again. This process of thinking is too in my head, and it is fighting with the anxiety that is mounting in my body. I close the door to my office, light a candle, and play a song by Silvia Nakkach entitled "Bliss" (2003). I take another deep breath and allow my body to begin to move very slowly, slow circles with my neck, hips, ankles, and wrists. I allow my spine to become more fluid, and then my knees and elbows join into the dance. I move through this dance where the only thing that I'm thinking of is my breath; no thoughts come to mind, my voice in my mind telling me to "write!" is not present in this moment. Now it is only my feet, my legs, my belly, my chest, and my arms, all moving together in this big dance. The song finishes but I continue to move for a few moments longer. It suddenly dawns on me that I had tried to sit down and write, and I hadn't activated my body. My mind was fully awake, but my body needed time to attune to the task of writing. My body had to not think to think.

When I approach my desk, I am struck by a thought. I sit down and the words begin to quickly appear on the screen. My thinking is now a dance between my mind and my body.

* * *

I've continued this dance through the course of writing this book. I consciously practiced *embodiment*, the act of being in one's body, to aid in writing *Somacultural Liberation*. This book is, after all, about the body.

Soma is the Ancient Greek word for body. When I write of the body, I refer to an *individual body* and a *collective body*. Culture plays a significant role in both. Individual body culture refers to our primary and secondary socializations and choices we make that impact how we see ourselves, and others, in the world around us. Collective body culture refers to group experiences that impact bodies. Some of us experience our personal and collective bodies in similar ways, depending on where we live and who we interact with most. Our individual body may feel comfort when we are around bodies that are similar to us in age, disability, religion, race, sexual orientation, socioeconomic status, nationality, and gender. Our body can also feel a sense of discomfort when we feel othered by a person or a group of people who see our difference as strange and unwelcome. One of the ways my body has both comfort and discomfort is around my identity as a mixed-race Native American. Being Native American in the United States is not just a racial category that one checks a box for. It is also a political statement, because Native Americans are the only racial group in the United States that must be able to prove their racial heritage. According to the United States government, unless you are an enrolled member of a Native American tribe (either federal or state recognized), you do not qualify to be called a Native American person.

I am an enrolled member of the Poarch Band of Creek Indians, a federally recognized sovereign nation located in the state now known as Alabama. As an adult, being able to check the Native American box on applications has worked to my advantage, yet as a child and teen, I suffered an immense identity complex because of the dual heritage that I was raised with. From a somatic perspective, there is the issue of my skin, which is not quite dark enough to read as Native to most people, yet not quite light enough to read as Caucasian. I'm most often told that I look Spanish, Puerto Rican, or Italian. When people learn that I was born and raised in North Dakota they almost always ask, "Are you Native American?" which they follow with the inevitable question, "How much?" I explain to them that my Indigeneity comes from my maternal family and I am Native to the southeastern region of the United States, Alabama. This is often followed with "Wow, I didn't know there were any Indians in Alabama."

When I look into the mirror I see my maternal grandmother's eyes and skin. I see the nose that sits on the face of all my aunts, my uncles, and my mother. I see the jaw that has been passed down through generations of trauma and abuse. I also see beyond my skin and feel the disease that stole my gallbladder at an early age, a common problem among Native American people and a rampant problem in my tribal community. I see beyond the color of my skin and see the historical legacy of shame that I carry on my shoulders based on not being able to communicate in my Native Muscogee language. My cultural and racial heritage are more than the markers that reside in my physical features; they are a testament to my fight for survival.

I do not identify with my Euro-American heritage and therefore I make the statement that my body doesn't either. Yet, I cannot deny this part of my being. It is there in the color of my hair. It is present in my lips, which are the same as my father's, and my wide chest, which is the same as my paternal grandfather's. It is present in my vocal development, the way that I inflect my tones and pronounce my vowels. It is a part of me; it is what makes me whole.

The way we feel about bodies, ours or others, varies depending on the cultural phenomena we are engaging with. This can be anything from weight, height, and hair color, and whether we have hair or not, to breast, vulva, penis, and butt size, and on and on. Characteristics of our bodies impact how comfortable we feel interacting with other bodies because bodies have culture, or rather, bodies have been assigned cultural attributes, generally by the dominant cultural group. As a penis-bodied person (this is a term I sometimes use to describe myself rather than male or masculine, which I do not always identify with), I understand penis size has cultural relevance including when people talk about sex, discuss how someone dresses or represents themselves, or trade stories or jokes in the locker room.

BODY STORY

His looked different from mine, not just the shaft, but also the entire area. His hair was thicker, darker. His scrotum hung lower, and his penis looked as if something were covering the head. I had never seen an uncircumcised penis before showering with Jeremy during physical education in ninth grade. Not only had I never seen an uncircumcised penis, but I also hadn't even known that some penises were not circumcised. After seeing Jeremy's uncircumcised penis, I began to think about my own body and how it was different from the other boys my age. I had given a lot of thought to how puberty was changing my body, but I hadn't given any to how puberty was changing other boys' bodies. I noticed Jeremy's body because his locker was next to mine in the locker room, so I saw him naked every day before and after gym class. Each day I found myself wanting to stare at his body and find our commonalities and our differences. At night when I would get home, I would think about Jeremy's naked body and I would examine my own body, sometimes in the mirror, and other times by exploring with my hands. I was fascinated by how my body could transform through thought and touch. Intrigued at the pleasure I could grant my body through touch. Full of wonder of the shifts I was experiencing in my body as I aged.

Curious to see how others were developing, I began to pay closer attention to the boys when we would shower together after gym class. Some were very developed for their age (we were about fourteen), and others looked as if they still hadn't begun puberty. It was about this time that I really began to question my sexuality. Was I curious about Jeremy's body for the sake of curiosity, or was I curious because I had started to develop sexual feelings for him?

We had gym class right before our lunch period. Showering was mandatory, and each boy, in sets of twos, had to work towel duty for two different weeks throughout the semester. Jeremy and I were assigned towel duty together, which also meant that we would not shower until all the other boys had finished and we had cleaned their towels up and put them in the hamper. On the second day of our towel duties, our P.E. teacher had to leave early and left us in charge of making sure the towels were sorted. After finishing our chore, Jeremy and I did as we normally did and went into the shower room. I remember feeling very insecure in the shower with just Jeremy. My body felt even more exposed, and I was worried that I might get an erection. After a few minutes Jeremy stated how weird it was for just the two of us to be in the shower room. I remember laughing shyly and feeling lightheaded. He then came over and started to talk to me about his penis. He told me that he had seen me looking at him. I started to deny what he was saying, but he then said that he looked at mine as well. He told me that he wished his penis looked like mine because he felt that his was funny looking compared to everyone else's. I told him that I thought his looked cool. He asked me if I wanted to touch it. I wanted to, I really wanted to, but I was too shy and told him no. He said no big deal and walked out of the shower room. For the remainder of our towel service duty, and the remainder of our time together in middle school and high school, Jeremy and I never spoke. Years later he approached me at a mutual friend's wedding and told me that he was bisexual and that he never forgot about that time in the shower room. He asked me if I wanted to take him up on his offer from years ago. I smiled, thanked him, and once again told him no.

* * *

My sexuality has been integral to how I understand my body. My body was teased and beaten because of how sexuality was projected onto me as a child and teenager. As a young adult, I would use my body and my sexuality to help pay my bills while living in New York City. In my early twenties I experienced a sexual assault that took me years to understand was not my fault because I felt as if I knowingly put myself in the position to be violated the way that I was. After all, I was paid to dance for them, and I was paid to be objectified by them. Each 30-minute set was an opportunity to make extra cash that I felt I needed to survive in New York so that I could support my desire to be an artist. "Dancing is art," I would tell myself, yet I hid my work from my family and most of my friends.

The stage gave me a rush of adrenaline; it always had. Being on stage that way was different only because of the amount of clothing that I wore and the music that played; it was still a performance. I was a dancer. I already recognized that it wasn't just the extra cash that kept me coming back; it was the way that I would feel while I was on stage—and afterward—that also contributed. When I was dancing, I didn't feel shame about my sexuality or my body; on the contrary, I felt powerful, sexy, and in control. I thrived on the money that was being given to me because of the fantasy that I was fulfilling for the patrons of the club, some strangers, but mostly regulars. I allowed myself to be objectified by them and, in turn, objectified myself.

I can still remember the color of my outfit the night that it happened, white. I liked wearing white because the color accentuated my body in all the right ways. I finished my time on the stage and made my way around the room to accept tips. I had seen this patron before, had even accepted tips from him in the past. Before I got to him, I could feel his eyes on me, and my instinct told me not to go toward him. I ignored the feeling of fear and made my way across the room. I remember smiling and saying hello. He wore a hat, cowboy shirt, jeans, and black boots. He didn't say anything to me, so I turned to walk away. He grabbed my arm and spun my body so that my back was against his chest. He put his arm across my throat and his other arm went forcibly down my underwear. I remember the feel of his hand yanking in a very aggressive manner against my genitals. I remember the pain in my throat and the lack of breath in my body. I remember his belt buckle pressing against my back. The fear, panic, and pain were real.

As I write this, I am aware that my heart is racing, and I have a feeling of nausea in my stomach. My shoulders feel heavy; I want to cry. My lower back is hurting; I feel the need to scream. I feel shame.

I had been working at the club for about a year prior to this incident. That was my last night as a go-go dancer.

* * *

I rarely think about that night anymore because it brings me to a place of discomfort with my body and my sexuality, which, when I really think about it, when I really feel it in my body, is how I felt the entire time I was go-go dancing. The dancing, the tips, the objectification all served as a mask for the pain that I was trying to cover in my body, mind, emotions, and spirit.

There is a saying: "The body never lies." I call BS on this expression because I know first-hand my body lies all the time, because the mind is part of the body, and the mind can do all kinds of sneaky and deceitful things to our system. Mindfulness teaches us the importance of slowing down, connecting with our breath, and leaning into the mind/body connection. Capitalism teaches us to reject the mind/body connection and cut our bodies off from our awareness. If our bodies feel pain or discomfort, capitalism teaches us there is a pill for that, or a cream, or something we can buy to feel better, or look better, or dissociate even more. I believe true mind/body connection is only possible when we recognize the power our mind has in manipulating our system. Sometimes the mind manipulates our system as a form of protection, to keep us safe. Other times the mind manipulates our system to feed the dopaminergic reward system (i.e., gambling, drugs, sex).

I believe culture plays a significant role in how we understand our relationship to our bodies and other bodies. Our bodies can feel immense constriction in certain situations such as when we are introduced to a new culture for the first time. Our bodies can also feel immense expansion in this same situation. The difference between the states of contraction and expansion will vary person to person depending on the cultural experiences they have had prior to a new culture or cultural experience being introduced to their system. I believe the way culture shapes and informs our bodily experiences is a fascinating thing.

2

CULTURE

When I say *somacultural*, I am referring to the body's relationship to culture, which I believe shapes and informs our bodily experiences. When I write of the *soma*, I am referring to both the individual body of one person and a collective of bodies that form a culture. Although certain bodies who share cultural experiences may have similar somatic experiences in relation to the culture they were raised in, or experienced later in their life, everybody will still experience their own somacultural experience.

I believe it is important that I share my operational definition of culture with you. *Culture* is a set of intersecting beliefs, ideas, practices, and values humans engage with and react to on personal, relational, and communal levels. Culture has also been anthropomorphized and placed upon members of the animal kingdom including primates, cetaceans, insects, and birds. One of the most important ways I define culture is that culture has been created by humans. Further, culture can be a tool of liberation, or a tool of oppression, depending upon who created it, how it was created, and how it is used as a justification for ecstasy or exile.

We see culture represented in our countries of origin, families of origin, and families of creation. Culture is further represented in the clothes we wear, the foods we eat, the media we consume, and the laws we enact. Different states and cities within the United States have different cultures too. Culture is fluid, changing over generations.

Culture can be appreciated or appropriated. *Cultural appreciation* is the practice of naming, acknowledging, and respecting where a cultural practice comes from. I also believe that to be in true cultural appreciation, you give financial compensation to the culture you may be profiting from. Examples of this may be giving back to a human rights organization in India if you are running a yoga center in the United States or giving financial compensation to a Native American tribe or human rights organization if you are now doing land acknowledgments as part of your corporate practice.

Cultural appropriation is the practice of taking a cultural practice and claiming it as your own, without any regard for the original culture it was taken from. Cultural appropriation includes taking cultural practices from a group or groups of people who were not allowed to practice their culture without fear of condemnation, suffering, imprisonment, or death. Cultural appropriation is also the practice of profiting off of a cultural practice or belief outside your own culture without recognizing or considering the original culture it was taken from. The US is rampant with cultural appropriation. Cultural appropriation is foundational to "American" culture. The US was founded and continues to thrive on cultural appropriation. Did you know the US Constitution was based upon practices of the Iroquois Confederacy? That's right, the United States was founded on cultural appropriation, while at the same time it normalized disregard for Indigenous beliefs, practices, and values. It was not until 1988 that the United States government recognized how the Iroquois Confederacy inspired the constitutional framers, including George Washington and Benjamin Franklin (H.Con.Res. 331, 1988).*

* This resolution, sponsored by Rep. M. K. Udall and the Committee on Interior and Insular Affairs, acknowledges "the contribution of the Iroquois Confederacy of Nations to the development of the United States constitution and to reaffirm the continuing government-to-government relationship between Indian tribes and the United States established in the Constitution." See Report to accompany H. con. res. 331, including the cost estimate of the Congressional Budget Office (1988). Washington, DC; US GPO.

Pop culture is also guilty of cultural appropriation. Elvis Presley is often credited with creating rock and roll, while no credit is given to the Black and Indigenous roots of rock music, especially Sister Rosetta Tharpe. Musical artists such as Madonna, Eminem, and Katy Perry have been accused of cultural appropriation, as has film director James Cameron for his *Avatar* films.

I recently had a conversation with some students I was teaching at a university in the Bay Area of California around cultural appropriation. We were discussing a few Native music groups, Snotty Nose Rez Kids and The Hallucination. These groups (which I really enjoy) utilize hip hop and electronic music in their work. The question that I posed to the students is whether or not Indigenous people in North and South America could be accused of cultural appropriation when they were forced to assimilate to a culture that was not theirs. I further asked how it was okay and expected for Indigenous people to appropriate White European culture (including religion and spoken English), yet be challenged for incorporating elements of Black culture into their art. The students had a variety of responses, with the Native students in my class arguing that Native people cannot be accused of cultural appropriation because there can be no cultural appropriation from a culture that has oppressed and continues to oppress them and that benefits financially off of their oppression. When discussing elements from other cultural groups, the Native students suggested Native people still practiced cultural appreciation and not appropriation because their land was taken, their culture diluted, and dominant cultural groups benefited from the genocide of their ancestors. The Native students also spoke to how they most closely identified with certain aspects of Black culture because of shared experiences of colonization and ongoing settler oppression.

In varying places in the United States differing cultural values become apparent. This includes values having to do with bodily autonomy—for instance, access to abortion and consenting adults giving or receiving certain sexual behaviors, such as anal sex. In the United States, geographies become labeled red or blue. Varying state and local governments in the US have sometimes imposed travel advisories limiting official government travel between certain states that have restrictive human rights practices, ideologies, and laws. The ongoing culture grievances between the binary of left and right exclude all of us who are perhaps nowhere on the binary because we exist in a spherical realm on intra- and interpersonal relationality.

People do not need to have the same positionality (which includes culture) to understand, love, create with, marry, have sex with, and/or celebrate with one another. If I understand my body's relationship to your body from my cultural references, and you understand your cultural references and their impact on your body in relation to my body, I believe it helps me be in a more empathetic relationship with you. This is particularly relevant when people from different age groups talk about generational differences. We must acknowledge that during certain time spans in history, certain cultural practices were normalized, which of course does not make them right, equal, or equitable. This history may impact how someone may think about certain language or a set of values. Additionally, we also need to take place into consideration. Place is a reference to land. Land does not just hold value, land holds values. The cultural foundation of colonized lands is based upon force, domination, and oppression as access points to controlling the original inhabitants of that land. We live in a culture of conscious unconsciousness.

Finally, I ask you to keep these terms in mind when you are thinking about culture: ethnocentrism and ethnorelativism. *Ethnocentrism* is the practice and belief that your culture is superior to other cultures. Ethnocentrism is synonymous with racism, homophobia, transphobia, xenophobia, misogyny, and religious intolerance. Ethnocentrism can be subtle or extreme. *Ethnorelativism* is the practice of seeing and believing that other cultures are as unique and as valuable as one's own.

CULTURAL CONFLICTS

One of the greatest misconceptions about culture is that it recognizes differences. I offer a reframe to this perspective. Culture recognizes uniqueness. That is a good thing. We are all unique. We are unique on individual levels and societal levels, and many people strongly believe in nationhood as a unique characteristic to their identity. I remember a cultural conflict I had a few years ago with a White, cis-straight male who pulled the "I don't see race" card and pointed to his Black wife as an example. When I asked him to clarify and he said there was nothing more to say, I asked if my being Native had any perspective shift for him. He said, "Why would it?" I said, "Because of colonization." He laughed. I left.

I used to belong to a private group on Facebook that was set up for Poarch tribal members. The forum was supposed to be a place where members could ask questions about issues impacting our tribal community, though it was largely used as a place for tribal members (and those who wanted to be enrolled) to complain. Politics was often a subject of discussion. I was always incredibly dumbfounded by tribal members who supported the presidency of Donald Trump. I do not understand how a Native person would vote for and continue to support someone or a group of elected officials who threaten tribal sovereignty. To have a culture clash within a specific culture is possible.

If I am reflective of my positionality and epistemology, I can see the uniqueness of a person. I have studied a lot about Native people and culture and have worked with and within Native community my entire life. I know that some of the tribal members on that Facebook page do not have the same level of or access to education that I do. I recognize it is important for me to understand how higher education shapes someone's perspective. I understand the link between who is elected to federal office and how that affects my tribal community's sovereignty because I have studied the subject matter in college. I now also teach American Indian Studies at the college level and am surrounded by brilliant Native scholars and activists who openly share their knowledge with me. I no longer participate in the Facebook group because I had several arguments with people that left me in states of dysregulation, anger, and sadness. One argument ended when I shared with the person that I believed we were having a cultural conflict not based upon our identities as Poarch Creek people. Our cultural conflict had to do with our political ideologies. I also shared that our cultural conflict was one of education as I was pursuing a PhD and had been introduced to various court cases, statistics, narratives, and research that informed my thinking and how I understand what I believe in. He saw me in a new way after I expressed that and thanked me for being one of the tribal members who used the education benefit available to all citizens for my tribal nation. He also shared that he understood that I have a different perspective because of what I know. The basis of our argument was not resolved. I didn't sway him to the side I was promoting, though we did leave on better terms. I will take leaving on better terms any day over holding a grudge or malice toward someone.

I do not believe that a cultural conflict is necessarily ethnocentric. Sometimes we have not been exposed to a certain culture or cultural experience and our systems may not know how to regulate to the experience as it is happening. Ethnocentrism is a kind of awareness. Cultural conflicts arise in ethnocentrism all the time and are part of the foundation. They go well together, and it is how you handle the cultural conflict that I believe is important. Cultural conflicts do not need to be worked out with the person, group, or entity that you do not agree with, though if you seek that route there are plenty of resources for doing so, such as talking through the issues, going to therapy, utilizing the legal systems, staging protests, and the dark routes of war and genocide.

Sometimes we can work out cultural conflicts on personal levels by understanding our own relationship to what is being evoked; this is where a somacultural framework can be useful. When I can understand and reflect on my personal experiences and the influences they have had on my understanding of the world I live in, I can create space for additional perspectives to be true for someone else. I do not need to agree with the person or people. I can vehemently disagree and still create space in my own system.

We live in a divided world based upon cultural conflicts, ethnocentrism, and the deleterious implications that arise when they intersect. To apply a somacultural liberatory framework means to strive for an ethnorelativism that honors the uniqueness in individual and collective cultures. This is not possible if we continue to inflict injustice, oppression, and incriminations on people who are just living their lives. From my perspective as a Two-Spirit person, we cannot heal until everyone is in the circle together. This is only possible when we recognize, support, uplift, and celebrate the uniqueness in one another. We need to do a lot more work to get to this point where we can all be in the circle together. Old ways of being and knowing need to change. Old ways of privilege and power need to change. Old ways of seeing difference instead of uniqueness need to change. I believe it starts on the individual level and reverberates from there.

For many people who identify as American, this change includes a process called *unsettling*. Unsettling refers to disturbing something. From a somacultural liberation framework, unsettling refers to being in active inquiry with one's relationship to colonization, settler ideologies, and the benefits and privileges that have come from the genocide of the Indigenous people and indentured servitude of Black people. I am in an unsettling process as well. As a mixed-race Native person with European ancestry, I am still learning what I didn't learn at home or at school. I have entered a state of recognizing that I have both suffered from and benefited from the injustices against Indigenous people and Black people. I understand racism on a personal, communal, and systemic level. I have experienced racism and I have undoubtedly thought, done something, or acted in a racist manner. To deny that would be to perpetuate my own ignorance. Some may argue that for something to be racist, it has to have inherent intention behind it because race plus power equals racism. I agree with this formula as one way racism is expressed. I also believe that in our broader American culture, we continue to normalize certain racist ideologies and perspectives, thus potentially making someone think, do, or say something that is racist. Ignorance is not an excuse for racist behavior.

One of my favorite quotes is from Maya Angelou who said, "Do your best until you know better. Then when you know better, do better." When we learn about the injustices Indigenous and Black people have experienced and continue to experience, we must do better. When we learn about the injustices experienced by our lesbian, gay, bisexual, trans, gender nonconforming, and intersex communities, we must do better. When we learn about the injustices that are done to minority groups including refugees, those living with HIV, those who are unhoused, and those who are living in poverty, we must do better.

Our cultural conflicts invite us to explore the parts of us that are disharmonious within ourselves, within our relationships to others, and within our relationship to the larger world and society. There is always opportunity for growth. Growth requires work, though it remains possible.

THE CULTURE OF SURVIVAL

A clear distinction needs to be made around cultural appropriation and cultural assimilation. As described earlier, *cultural appropriation* is extracting culture and using it to benefit an individual or a group of people outside of the original culture it was created in, primarily for financial gain. *Cultural assimilation* differs from cultural appropriation because it is when an individual or group of people accept dominant cultural practices and ideologies. The United States is often considered a melting pot of cultures, and although certain aspects of this are true, we should also recognize that the US is an assimilation of minority cultures into the dominant White American culture. Nowhere is this more apparent than in religion and language.

We have been fed an origin story about the US being founded on religious freedom. Yet religion, specifically Christian religion, continues to be one of the primary cultural assimilation tools that upholds a particular set of values. An example of this is the abundance of Native American people who practice some form of Christianity, whether Catholicism or varying denominations of the Christian faith. Since the invasion of the lands we now call the United States (including Alaska and Hawaii), colonizers have forced Native people to assimilate to the Christian faith or face hardships and even death. Beginning with the Civilization Fund Act of 1819 and the Peace Policy of 1869, boarding schools were established in the United States to "kill the Indian, save the man," a quote attributed to Richard Henry Pratt. Pratt's idea was to remove Native people from the "cultural savagery" they lived in and Americanize them by forcing them to speak English, wear European fashion, and become Christians. Boarding schools were also implemented in Canada.

By the 1920s over 80 percent of Native American children attended boarding schools, primarily without choice (Callimachi, 2021). Boarding schools did not consider that the Native children they were assimilating came from different Native tribal communities and had unique cultural differences, including language. When Native children did not follow the assimilation guidelines they were being forced to accept, they were punished, beaten, and sexually assaulted. Thousands of bodies of Native

American children in the US and Canada have been found in unmarked graves at former boarding school sites. These schools were primarily run by Catholic and other Christian denominations, with funding coming directly from the US government. The Catholic church and other Christian churches have never been held accountable for the mass murders and abuses they committed against Native children. Pratt's moniker to "kill the Indian" was taken literally by those running boarding schools. In the US 367 boarding schools operated, and in Canada there were 139 (Goodyear, 2021). Please note, these numbers only include government-supported boarding schools and do not account for any independent boarding schools that may also have been operating. These boarding schools, as horrific and violent as they were, did as Pratt intended; they assimilated Native people into the dominant White American culture.

The Bureau of Indian Education, a subsidiary of the US government, currently operates 183 schools for Native children, primarily non-boarding and based on reservations. Although the stated intent of these ongoing boarding schools is to prepare Native students for higher education and to enter the workforce, assimilation is the true primary motivator. I encourage you to learn more about the injustice Native children experienced through the boarding school system, and the ongoing efforts, including holding the Catholic church accountable, to bring justice to those who suffered and died to fulfill Pratt's zealous ambition.

For Native people who survived the boarding school era, the US further incentivized assimilation with the Indian Relocation Act of 1956, also known as Public Law 959, which was an extension of the termination policy the US government enacted beginning in 1953. The Indian Relocation Program was billed as a vocational training program, with the intention of moving Native people off of reservations and assimilating them into the general population. Through the Indian Relocation Program, thousands of Native individuals and families moved off of the reservation and into large urban areas including Los Angeles, San Francisco, New York, Chicago, Denver, Minneapolis, and Seattle. For many of these individuals and families the Indian Relocation Program was a one-way ticket from reservation poverty to urban poverty, with many of the promises of the program going unfulfilled. The Indian Relocation Program was not a benefit to Native American people; rather it was another failed policy of the US government to assimilate Native people and terminate the Native way of life. The impact the program had on Native people continues to this day.

While not an intention of the Indian Relocation Program, Native people from different tribal communities began to organize, and it is through these efforts we see the beginnings of intertribal or pantribal Native activism efforts, including the American Indian Movement (AIM), which was founded in 1965 in Minneapolis. AIM chapters began to appear in urban cities across the US and were in part responsible for the occupation of Alcatraz in San Francisco from November 1969 to June 1971.

The culture of survival exists within every marginalized group of people, or marginalized person. It is important to remember that someone can be marginalized while continuing to belong to and/or benefit from membership in a dominant cultural group. Every person who grew up in an abusive home will understand the culture of survival. What I mean by the *culture of survival* is adapting certain body postures and body practices to blend in, to make oneself small, and living in a hypervigilant state. Living in such a state is to live in a state of constriction, always readying for an attack of some kind. Sometimes hypervigilance is easy to spot. Many men who identify as gay or homosexual live in a hypervigilant state, with some going as far as to armor their bodies with muscle to appear bigger and to give themselves a sense of safety so others (the oppressors) are less likely to target them. I have seen this in my clinical practice countless times.

In my work as a psychotherapist who specializes in issues impacting the body (somatic psychology), I have been trained to watch people's bodies as they share their stories and work toward healing the challenges affecting their lives. Many of my clients will do what I call a chair dance when they are feeling anxious. I will see their feet moving around; I will see them shifting their weight from side to side, tapping their fingers, or gently swaying. They often accompany this with their breath. When clients are feeling angry or defensive, I often see them cross their arms, puff out their chest, and clench their jaw. The body is a marvel at adapting to emotions the system is experiencing. When I call attention to the chair dance or the defensive arm posture, most times clients will not recognize they are doing anything with their bodies at all. I do not fault them for disconnecting from their body as I believe the culture of survival is so deeply ingrained in all of our systems and so many of us are living in our heads, cut off from the sensations in our body that alert us to dysregulation and danger.

Every client I have worked with falls somewhere along an anxiety spectrum. Where they land could be a potential clinical diagnosis, or mild anxiety that is occasionally problematic. Anxiety impacts everybody differently. Some people experience anxiety as an overall body sensation of constriction, tightness, tingling, and breathing abnormalities (hyperventilation or holding the breath for long periods). Other clients experience anxiety as fogginess in the brain, lack of sexual function, or inability to speak. In my practice all of these clients share something in common, the desire to rid anxiety from their lives. Not possible, I tell them. We need anxiety. While we don't need anxiety in extreme states that paralyze our systems, we do need to be made aware of life-threatening situations that put our bodies, or other bodies, beloved animals, homes, and the like in imminent danger. Anxiety is an adaptive strategy, an internal alarm system, that has been encoded in our systems an evolutionary strategy for survival. Anxiety helps us survive.

Experiential: Culture Writing Prompt

What do you know about your culture? When you hear the phrase *your culture,* what comes to mind? Take 10 minutes and write about your culture as you understand it. Try to write in a free-verse style, meaning write whatever comes to mind without pausing. If you'd rather, you could instead set a timer for 10 minutes and either write or speak aloud and record yourself reflecting on the culture you were raised in and any culture or cultural practices you have created or participated in outside of that culture.

3

LIBERATION

Every liberation movement in the past, in the present, and in the future is about the body. Liberation movements, whether they are attached to antiracism, women's rights, 2SLGBTQIA+ rights, or religious freedoms, exist because bodies have been oppressed. Throughout human history, stories of humans oppressing other humans' bodies have existed. These stories exist across the globe and are not limited to any specific region or country. Examples include the genocide of the Indigenous people and the enslavement of African people in the Americas, the Holocaust in Europe, the caste system in India, and the colonization of Australia and Asia. Although these examples may differ in regard to what has and continues to happen, they all share one thing in common, the human body.

Oppression requires coercion of the body; thus, liberation requires freeing the body. My belief of somacultural liberation requires acknowledging that all bodies are not treated equally. Although written history has always favored the story of the oppressors, liberation will always favor the oppressed. This begs the question of whether the oppressor can ever find or feel liberation. I believe the answer can only be yes if the oppressor is willing to acknowledge the pain and harm they have caused others and is willing to recognize and rectify the benefits they have received (either directly or intergenerationally) by their acts of oppression.

In my birth country, the United States, there are constant reminders of the genocide of the Indigenous people and the colonial rule Indigenous people continue to live under. Some of these reminders are embodied by the American military complex and the reservation system. Although Indigenous people have served in the US military forces for over two hundred years, they did not gain US citizenship until 1924 with the passage of the Indian Citizenship Act signed by President Calvin Coolidge. Indigenous people, and in particular Dine (Navajo) people, have been rightfully credited with helping the US military complex win WWII. Still, many Indigenous people feel serving in the US military perpetuates ongoing colonial abuse both in the US and abroad.

One of the greatest ironies of the US origin story is that of religious liberation. We have been sold an origin story that the United States was founded on the value of religious freedom. Yet Indigenous people did not gain religious freedom until 1978 with the passing of the American Indian Religious Freedom Act. Do you catch the irony of a country being founded on religious freedom (Doctrine of Discovery and Manifest Destiny), while using religion to commit genocide against the original inhabitants of the land? Religious freedom in the US has long been a tool used to oppress minorities including to enslave African people and deny the rights to 2SLGBTQIA+ people.

It is dangerous to talk about liberation. Many of our cherished icons know that all too well. In any of our cultural backgrounds, we have leaders who have been the targets of violence because they attempted to help free their families, loved ones, and community members from ongoing assaults on autonomy, sovereignty, and freedom. No doubt, you have also experienced violence–physical, mental, emotional, sexual, lateral, spiritual, and so on—that has led you to seek your own liberation. Maybe you also intend to help others attain their liberation. Māori activist Lila Watson is credited as having said, "If you have come here to help me, you are wasting your time. But if you have come here because your liberation is bound with mine, then let us work together." I am writing this book, and sharing parts of my journey along the way, because I believe what

Lila Watson said. I believe that if I am to be truly free, I must work with others on this collective path of healing and liberation so that we can all get closer to freedom. Somacultural liberation does not exist in a solitary field. It is a multidirectional process of sharing and experiencing pleasure, and pleasure heals. Somacultural liberation is one path to returning to ourselves.

Although not all those who benefit from liberation experience pain and suffering, we must recognize that a group of people have always suffered, and sometimes died, for the liberation of others. Social justice leaders Martin Luther King Jr. and Malcolm X were assassinated for their efforts in liberating Black Americans. Rigoberta Menchú was exiled from her home in Guatemala for her efforts to organize Indigenous resistance against Latin influence. Harvey Milk was assassinated for his work fighting for equality of LGBTQIA+ people. Sacheen Littlefeather was blacklisted in Hollywood for her activism on the Oscars' stage protesting the treatment of Native Americans by the film and television industry. Viola Liuzzo, an American civil rights activist, was assassinated by members of the Ku Klux Klan. Gauri Lankesh, an Indian journalist, was assassinated outside of her home in Bangalore for her opposition to right-wing Hindu extremism.

This list could go on for page and pages. All of these people sacrificed their bodies for the liberation of other bodies. Perhaps the most well-known example of this in Western culture is Jesus Christ, who is said to have died for the sins of humanity to bring all of us closer to God. Again, the irony of Christ's sacrifice is not without notice as his act ended up being the justification for Manifest Destiny and the genocide of millions of Indigenous people across the globe and the enslavement of African and Indigenous people to benefit White Europeans. I have never read a teaching of Jesus in which he advocates for using his name to inflict harm upon others.

My work as an activist has always focused on liberation. I advocate for the liberation of Indigenous people. I advocate for the liberation of 2SLGBTQIA+ people. I advocate for women's rights, including trans women. I advocate for healthcare for all people, including access to sexual healthcare, abortion, and lifesaving medication. My work has been criticized as being out of touch with reality. "Whose reality?" I ask. If I am out of touch with the reality of the oppressor, that is exactly my point. We live in a world in which only a few are ever granted certain rights, while millions of others suffer. We cannot be liberated as a species, as a society, as a culture unless all of us are liberated. What can we do to ensure this will happen? Keep breathing, of course; the rest will evolve. I also recommend starting with the self. I believe we can work toward collective and individual liberation. I believe somacultural liberatory ideology is one of many ways in which someone can become closer to liberation. I will take being closer to liberation over never taking any steps toward freedom.

4

HOW WE KNOW WHAT WE KNOW

POSITIONALITY

In the first year of my PhD studies, I was given an article, "How Does Your Positionality Bias Your Epistemology?" by David Takacs (2003). The article focused primarily on classroom education, though I believe it was one of the most transformative articles I had ever read in my fifteen-year education journey. This article helped shift my knowledge (epistemology) and I began to apply what I was learning to who I was for perhaps the first time in my life (positionality). Takacs writes, "knowledge does not arrive unmediated from the world; rather, knowledge gets constructed by interaction between the questioner and the world" (p. 31). My interpretation of this quote gave me an opportunity to question all the parts of myself that I allowed to show up in learning environments, which in my world were many.

When I first read the Takacs article, in addition to being a PhD student, I was also a psychotherapist and sex therapist in private practice. I was interacting with my clients and the questions they posed to their worldview every time I was in session with them. This one quote helped me to further recognize the influence a client's cultural experiences had on the ways they understood their experiences—somatically, intellectually, and emotionally. It also helped me understand myself in a new way. I learned that my own cultural experiences had created the knowledge that I carried with me and how this knowledge shaped who I was and how I chose to interact with the world around me.

I have been engaging with the Takacs article for many years and the article is mandatory reading for any course that I teach, whether it is an undergraduate course, a graduate course, or part of a workshop or sex therapy/sex educator certification course that I am leading. The article is also one of the foundations of inspirations that I have used in conceptualizing this book.

My knowledge is based upon the culture that I was born into, was introduced to, and created on my own accord. The traumas and the triumphs I have experienced personally, interpersonally, and in micro- and macro-sociocultural contexts also add to my knowledge base. I resonate with Takacs (2003), who wrote, "When we develop the skill of understanding how we know what we know, we acquire a key to lifelong learning" (p. 29). Takacs talked about the applicability of positionality and epistemology from an education/classroom perspective and dynamic. Since my work was relating to therapy, I knew it was the meaning people made/believed/felt about their positionality and epistemology that was important to explore from a clinical perspective. Since we all come from and have culture, incorporating a deeper understanding of self is imperative in the foundation of somacultural liberation. Throughout this book, I share personal stories, thoughts, and reflections in the hope that my openness and vulnerability may inspire you to do some inner reflective growth-work as well. I have found the deeper inner reflective work to be incredibly healing.

* * *

My body likes to move. I feel my best when I am engaged in a daily movement practice of some kind: singing, cycling, practicing yoga, dancing, walking, and so on. When I do not have an opportunity to move my body in a way that helps regulate my system, I feel an imbalance in my body, mind, and spirit. Specific cultural ideations are attached to movement. Certain movements are associated more with binary gender correlations. Men lift weights, women do Pilates. It makes me laugh out loud even writing this statement because I know this is not true from my experience. I detest lifting weights, though I absolutely love doing Pilates. When I take a Pilates class at my local studio in the Castro neighborhood of San Francisco, I am often the only penis-bodied person in the room. I use the term penis-bodied when I am in shared spaces because I do not know, nor do I assume, any person's gender, other than my own, unless they have shared with me how they identify. This is a cultural shift that I have experienced after working in the sexuality field for many years. What value does it add to our society and larger American culture when we place movement in binary classifications? Is this tied to the ideology that strength and aggression require masculine energy, and care and compassion require feminine energy? Shortly, you will read about Two-Spirit people and how we are in balance with all the gender energies that exist in the world. Yes there are more than two. If you refuse to believe this, I ask you to sit with what it means to impose a cultural ideology onto a group of people who have existed long before the colonization of the North American continent. There may be only two genders according to colonizers. Indigenous people know differently, however, and we have always welcomed and made space for our gender-variant tribal members.

Throughout this book, I share my positionality including some of the challenges I have experienced due to my intersecting identities. My positionality includes being born to a Native American mother of Poarch Creek ethnicity and a White father of German-Russian ethnicity. My positionality also includes my identity as a Two-Spirit person, a term used by Indigenous people to signify gender and sexual orientation variance. I believe it is important to center myself in my work, because who I am is my primary source of what I know. I also believe it is important that you understand where my thinking comes from. If you understand who I am, I believe it can help you better understand yourself. Although we may not be able to change history, we can have an impact on the present moment and the future. My positionality and epistemology inspired

Somacultural Liberation, and I hope this book inspires you as well. As Lila Watson said, "Let us work together." I add to this sentiment and say, let us learn together.

ONE GESTURE

For the past two decades, I have dedicated my personal and professional life to the pursuit of healing. Because I came from a childhood and adolescence riddled with trauma, I knew that if I didn't heal, I was likely to fall into the same path of addiction that plagued both sides of my family. For years I tirelessly fought depression and anxiety and kept myself preoccupied with an endless pursuit of goals and activities that seemed beyond my reach, thus propelling me to work harder, longer, more rigidly, and unfortunately more stubbornly. I achieved all the academic accolades, associate's, bachelor's, master's, and PhD. Part ambition, part driven by shame, my attempt to quell the pain of feeling less than my peers led me to seek solace in achievements that mattered little to anyone beside myself.

* * *

I spent the first half of my life in conditions that were near poverty. Money was fleeting as was my sense of safety. My childhood was spent on the farm my father inherited from his father and his father before him. Though we had a roof over our heads and food on our table, my father's penchant for alcohol meant he prioritized numbing his demons over caring for his family, and he took his rage out on his family through verbal, emotional, and physical abuse. My mother, a high school dropout, lived in fear of my father's abuse and rage and of him leaving her to take care of her children on her own. Many times, she told me how sorry she was for not leaving my father sooner than she did. The catalyst for my parents' breakup was my mother witnessing me bloodied from a beating my father gave to me that left a scar on my face and deep trauma in my body and soul.

I look back at that moment, seeing my mother's eyes widen in horror, as the gesture that forever changed our lives. This one gesture, my mother's eyes literally opening, is the reason I believe I am alive to write these words today. The night of the worst beating I received in my life was also the night I began to recognize liberation was possible. My mom left my father that night. Even though they eventually got back together, their relationship didn't last, and my mother no longer allowed my father to manipulate and control her life. That one gesture changed her life as well.

Flash forward some thirty-five years later: I now work as a psychotherapist specializing in sex therapy, grief, and trauma. My work is centered on somacultural liberation. As you may recall, I use this phrase to emphasize my belief that our body is shaped and informed by our cultural experiences. These experiences exist on a primary and secondary socialization level. Think of *primary socialization* as your early childhood experiences with your parents, siblings, family members, or your primary caregivers, whomever they may have been. Our primary socializations also include the race, gender, sexual orientation, socioeconomic status, and any disabilities we have been living with (or that have been projected onto us in the case of gender) from our primary caregivers. *Secondary socializations* are the experiences you have outside of your family or primary caregivers, such as school, church, and exposure to other cultural aspects outside of your primary socialization. Also, think of these secondary socializations as how others perceive aspects of your identity. For example, I didn't think anything about being biracial and bicultural until others began to point it out and make me experience shame around these aspects of my life that I had no control over.

I believe understating the somacultural aspects of our lives gives us what we need to begin to heal the parts of our stories that continue to cause us pain. Being in relationship with this understanding helps us move away from the why and into the how. Time and time again, I hear clients ask why something has happened to them, why they feel the way they feel, and why they can't move on from the traumatic or challenging areas of their life. Living in the why is a defensive posture. By this I mean wondering why doesn't require us to lean in; rather, it creates tension in the body, making us pull way. When we ask how, we lean in, curious about the potential that lies before us.

Take a moment and try this out for yourself. Think back to a disagreement you have had with someone. Regardless of what the disagreement was about, remember how you may have felt if you said (or if it was said to you), "Why did you do this?" In this case, we are immediately on the defense, pulling away and dissociating, thus creating an even greater rupture. During any kind of disagreement, *why* often leads us to challenge back with "Because you. . . ." This reaction means that now everyone is upset and in a defensive posture. *Why* creates tension in the body. When we are tense, we constrict, we hold our breath, we dysregulate our sympathetic nervous system. This dysregulation can lead us to the states of fight, flight, freeze, fawn, or flop. It is in these states that trauma can take root.

Another state can also impact our sympathetic nervous system—that of curiosity. It is in this state that my interest in somacultural liberation began. Prior to my studies in counseling psychology and human sexuality, I studied cultural anthropology. Between readings on phylogeny and archeology, I took a course on human evolution. It was there that I first learned about our hominid ancestor *Australopithecus afarensis*, a species that is believed to have been the first to experience bipedalism, walking on two legs. What anthropologists are uncertain of is what led *Australopithecus afarensis* to adopt bipedal locomotion. Perhaps it was curiosity, an excitement of looking across the savanna and wondering what lay beyond the horizon. Perhaps it was a strategy to ward of predators as a tactic of survival. Whatever the reason, that one gesture changed the course of history and created a somacultural liberation framework that we can all use to follow our curious hearts and continue to seek our own freedom.

WHO I AM AND HOW I KNOW WHAT I KNOW

How did I get here, writing this book for all of you (and myself)? Although I think I have had many one-gesture moments throughout my life, a recent one sticks out in my somacultural experience the most. I was living in San Francisco, working toward my doctoral degree in human sexuality. It was the summer of 2018, and the San Francisco Pride parade was about to take place. I had planned to march with a group that I had been a part of since I first arrived in the Bay Area (Ohlone territory) in 2012, the Bay Area American Indian Two-Spirits

(BAAITS). I was the chair of the BAAITS board at the time, and one of my responsibilities was organizing our contingency for the parade. The night before the parade I told my husband, Sean, that I wanted to make a sign that said Decolonize Sexuality. I went to a local catch-all store, Cliff's, in the Castro neighborhood of San Francisco and purchased a white poster board, a set of stencils, and a thick black Sharpie marker. I spent several hours that night making the sign.

The day of the parade, I marched along Market Street in downtown San Francisco with my Decolonize Sexuality sign high above my head. I heard many people hooting and hollering for me and the sign as I made my way down the crowded parade route. I heard shouts of "Yes!" "Awesome!" "Decolonize!" that filled my heart with an immense sense of pride. I also heard a few people shout out "What does that mean?" prompting me to shout back "Figure it out!" Honestly, I wasn't exactly sure what I meant by the phrase; I just knew that it was relevant to the way I felt about my doctoral studies in human sexuality and my work as a psychotherapist and sex therapist.

A few months later I was helping organize the annual BAAITS Two-Spirit powwow, where we saw an average of five thousand attendees over the course of our one-day community event. I decided to take my Decolonize Sexuality sign with me to the powwow and display it at the welcome and information booth. That year, our powwow was covered by the *San Francisco Chronicle*, and in their article my poster got a shout-out. I knew that I was on to something. My research and academic studies took a turn, and I began to focus on the impact of colonization on Indigenous sexuality. In the following San Francisco Pride parade, I again took my Decolonize Sexuality sign with me and carried it proudly above my head as I marched down Market Street with BAAITS. Again I heard the encouraging exclamations and the familiar questions about what the sign meant. I was also interviewed by a local TV channel and given a shout-out by SFGATE who credited my Decolonize Sexuality sign as one of their most creative signs (Bartlett & Tran, 2019).

I was thrilled by all the attention and have since had many opportunities to share my message with several universities, sex therapy training sessions, and sexuality organizations.

My efforts to decolonize sexuality are many years in the making. Understanding how decolonizing and unsettling impacts my life is something that is still in process and likely it will continue to be throughout my time on Mother Earth. Part of how I understand the concepts of decolonizing and unsettling sexuality has to do with how I understand the somacultural aspects of my own identity.

* * *

I was born in the year of the American bicentennial, 1976, to a White Euro-American father of German-Russian ethnicity and a Native American mother of Poarch Creek (Muscogee also known as Mvskve) ethnicity. The timing of my birth is of note because, at the time, the Trail of Self Determination that was moving across the United States, and the first LGBTQIA+ Native American group, Gay American Indians, had just been formed by Randy Burns (Northern Paiute) and Barbara Cameron (Standing Rock Lakota Sioux) in 1975. As I've said previously, I identify as a mixed-race Native American of European descent. My name, Roger Kuhn, speaks only to the blood of the colonizer that runs through my veins. My name offers no indication that I also carry the blood of the colonized. My identity as a mixed-race Native American of European descent would be lost if I were only to be recognized by the Germanic origins of my name. In addition to being European American, I am Muscogee and an enrolled member of the Poarch Band of Creek Indians. The Poarch Band of Creek Indians is a sovereign nation with a direct government-to-government relationship with the United States. I am told I am *hotvlkvke* (wind clan). I am told I am *ennvrkvpv*, a Muscogee word that translates to "in the middle" and is being used by Two-Spirit Muscogee people and their allies in the Southeast region of the United States on and near the Poarch Creek Indians Reservation and on or near the Muscogee Nation reservation in Oklahoma.

One of the greatest challenges in my life has been understanding and reflecting upon what it means to be a person of mixed-race identity. Someone who has the blood of the colonizer and colonized running through me. The blood of the oppressor and the oppressed running through me. The blood of the rapist and the raped running through me. The blood of the murderer and the murdered running through me. I sit with these thoughts often. It's very uncomfortable. I situate myself in my mixed-race identity and my Indigeneity to recognize and draw attention to my positionality as it reflects on decolonization and unsettling.

I was raised in a predominately White culture. For the majority of my childhood, my mother, siblings, and I were the only non-White people in the small farming community of Napoleon, ND, located on occupied Očhéthi Šakówiŋ territory. We lived on a farm that had been in my father's family for several generations. I look back at my time on the farm with a mix of nostalgia, sorrow, and fear. I had many amazing adventures there, including countless hours exploring the land, singing with nature, and escaping from the reality of what waited for me back in the house. My father, Gary, was an abusive alcoholic who often made racist comments to my mother and me and ridiculed me for being effeminate. Though my father relished the fact that he married a Native American woman, he did not want his children to identify as Native and told me to tell people that I was only White/German. This wasn't as easy for me as it was my sisters, who have both a lighter complexion than I do and blue eyes. All my life I have had people ask me what my racial and ethnic background is. Being racially and ethnically ambiguous has always been a challenge. Depending on where I am in the world, I have people speak to me in a language other than English, thinking that I am from their ethnic/racial group. I recall a time when I was working in New York City (Lenape territory) when a small group of Spanish tourists chastised me for not speaking the Spanish language. They shouted at me to "learn my culture."

In Napoleon, I was teased on the playground for being mixed race. When my White grandparents and father were upset with my behavior, they said that it was the "wild Indian in me" that was being problematic. I learned not to talk about my Native identity and to assimilate into Whiteness as much as I could in order to avoid being made fun of. I hated it and struggled with finding some kind of balance to my identity. My mother did a similar thing in her life, assimilating to Whiteness in her youth. Her three marriages were all to White men. I have never identified as a White person. I have always identified as Native American, a cultural value my mother instilled in me at an early age. I also have never denied being mixed race and having a White father. When I do public speaking engagements, if I am speaking to majority White audiences about Native issues, I always joke with them to not worry because I speak White fluently.

My childhood also coincided with the beginning of the HIV pandemic, which continues to decimate people's lives. In childhood, I learned love and sex were dangerous and gay men did not deserve love because they were dirty and diseased (Buchanan, 1987). I also experienced countless instances of teasing and abuse from my father and other kids at school. My dad used to call me "femme," "sissy," "little faggot," usually right before he hit me. When I was in elementary school, I participated in gymnastics and was the only "boy" in the program. The high school wrestling team used to taunt me when I would come into the gym to practice. I was only ten years old. In high school one of my science teachers commented on my skin color in front of the class. The summation of her comments, and I am paraphrasing here, was that because I had a darker skin color than everyone in the class, I would be the most targeted for mosquito attacks. All the kids laughed, I felt humiliated. Another time in high school, a fellow student wrote a gay pejorative on my classroom folder, which was stored in a shared filing cabinet. I remember going to get my folder and seeing the words *Fag, Fag, I Suck Dick* written in big black ink letters. I did not tell the teacher; I don't think he would have cared.

Things shifted a bit for me when a student who had been harassing me for a few years was expelled from school for bringing a gun with him. When I heard that story, I couldn't help but think that I was probably one of his intended victims. With him gone, though, I did find a greater sense of ease in my body while I was at school.

There was another student who used to harass me a lot, especially while I was in math class, which was my hardest subject and one I was already dangerously close to failing. My teacher never did or said anything to him when he would say something rude, bullying, homophobic, or racist to me. She just kept teaching. One day we were learning a lesson I did not understand. I needed to concentrate, and the harassing student was up to his antics again. I had had enough of his taunts, and with a new sense of ease in my body, I blurted out loud with a thunderous voice,

"Shut the Fuck Up!" The entire room grew quiet. I stared at him with as much anger as I could; his mouth was agape and I could see his face getting flushed. The teacher sent both of us to see the principal. When I got into the principal's office (who happened to be my homeroom teacher and someone I had always found to be a kind, though strict, person), I unleashed on the student, the teacher, and the school in general for not providing a safe place for me to learn. The student never harassed me again and even apologized. A few years later, I would get into a small car accident and rear-end my old high school principal/homeroom teacher. When he got out of his car and saw that it was me, he gave me a hug and said he hoped I was doing all right in life.

While I was being harassed at school, I was also being harassed and abused at home. My parents eventually separated when I was thirteen, though the harassment from my father continued throughout my teen years. On one occasion he was enraged at me for not having fixed a leaking water pipe that I had no idea how to fix. He made me go under the house with him to check out the leak. When he himself was unable to fix the leak, he took it out on me. He hit me and told me it was time to grow up and be a man. Though I still feared him, something came over me that day and I spoke back to him for the first time in my life. I told him if he ever fucking touched me again, it would be the last time he did so. I was fifteen years old.

Our relationship became completely fractured the following summer when he offered me $1,000 to do some work for him on the family farm. Needing the money, and already plotting my exit strategy from North Dakota, I accepted his offer. One evening he came home drunk and confronted me for not being like him. He became violent and broke the lock on my bedroom door. He pulled me by my shirt collar and tried to throw me down the stairs. I managed to find my footing and ran out of the house. He followed in a rage and screamed at me to get back there and listen to him. I kept my distance, certain that I could outrun him if needed. Though the nearest farm was over a mile away, I knew that if I showed up at the neighbor's home, they would protect me. Thankfully it never came to that. My father went back into the house. About an hour later I came back inside and found him sitting at the kitchen table. He asked me to sit down and talk. Out of fear, I agreed and listened to my father divulge years of secrets about his life.

After about an hour and with the sun beginning to rise, he went into the living room and passed out. I ran upstairs, grabbed my belongings, and drove away from the farm; I didn't return until after his death.

Before he died, I wrote him what I call a fuck-you letter. I admonished him for what he told me and told him that I hated him, and I hoped to never see him again. I had already moved to New York City at this point in my life. I was surprised when, a few weeks after I sent my letter, my father called to apologize for all the pain he had caused me. He told me that I was right, that he was a bad person and an even worse father. He didn't sound drunk, though I have no idea if he had any drinks before he called. I thanked him for the call and said I would work on forgiving him, though I wasn't ready to say those words yet. Three months later, my father died from a drunk-driving car accident. I was twenty-three years old.

I had spent my life up to that point believing that my father would one day kill me, my mother, or my siblings. His violence and aggression were relentless. I did not know all of the demons my father was struggling with, though I knew that he had chosen to take them out on our family. It may seem crass to some readers that I speak of my father in this manner without him being able to defend himself. Truth be told, I couldn't care less what other people think of the abuse I experienced in my life because of my father. I do not need you to believe me because I know it is true. I experienced it firsthand and am often reminded of his violence when I see the scars on my body that were inflicted by his hands.

When I received the news of my father's death, I was working for an advertising agency in New York City. My oldest sister, Tammy, called me to deliver the news. I remember my sister's voice on the other end, asking if I was sitting down. Sister, calling at 10 a.m. East Coast time. What could she possibly want? "Dad's dead," she said. "Rog, are you there?" Dead, as in ding-dong the witch is dead. Dead, as in stiff as a board, six feet under, out of commission. Dead, as in the nightmare is over.

I needed to vomit. I left my desk and ran for the bathroom. Thank God I was alone. Moving into the bathroom stall, I dry heaved several times; nothing came up, I had skipped breakfast again. Dead, yes, she said he was dead. I sat on the toilet and chewed the nail of my right ring finger until it began to bleed, but I didn't feel any pain, just a light metallic taste in my mouth. My body began to shake; I needed to scream.

* * *

Flashback—I'm eleven years old walking home through the field, trailing my father by a few feet. I am tired, covered in mud and blood. It is difficult for me to keep up with him; I never realized he walked so fast. My back is hurting from the barbed wire that sliced my skin only moments ago. We arrive back at the house, and he tells me that I am to go downstairs and clean up. In the bathroom I relive the terror of his fists again. "It was an accident," I kept telling him, "I didn't mean to get the tractor stuck." The field was wet; it had rained. He didn't care. I was to blame. The first fist made me fall off the tractor; the second fist buried me in the mud. The third fist had me screaming for air; the fourth fist silenced me. I look into the bathroom mirror, his words clinging to my mind, "Clean yourself up." Yes, this is what my life has become. Beaten, bullied, bruised. Living in terror. Believing that one day he'll get drunk enough to make good on his promise to use his guns. I look into the mirror, face swollen, covered in blood. "No more," I hear a voice say. "No more." This is my voice. Small, meek, but resilient. No more.

I don't clean myself up. I walk upstairs and make eye contact with my mom. My mother immediately runs to my side and begins to cry. She starts to scream at my father and my parents fight like I have never seen before.

My sister tells me that I fainted and started to convulse. I remember waking up cradled in my sister Diva's arms shaking, begging to be taken away.

* * *

The flashback fades and I come out of the bathroom stall at the advertising agency. I am still alone, and I look into the mirror. I see the eleven-year-old boy I once was, covered in mud and blood. I touch the scar below my lip that serves as a reminder of the day I finally took a stand for my own safety. Ding-dong the witch is dead.

* * *

The night before the funeral we held a wake, and as I witnessed my father's body lying in the casket, I felt rage engulf my body. I didn't believe he suffered enough. I wanted his death to be long, slow, painful, and lonely. I thought of his mother, my grandma Elda who died of stomach cancer, and how much I loved her. I heard her voice in my head telling me it was going to be okay. I felt overwhelmed with emotion and needed to step away from the extended family and their sentiments of comfort and sorrow. They kept saying, "I'm sorry for your loss." I was not sorry. I felt no sorrow. I left the main room and found a small closet to hide in. My aunt Bonnie, my father's youngest sister and my favorite of his siblings, found me in the closet crying and told me it was okay to be sad. I told her I wasn't crying because I was sad, I was crying because I finally felt free.

With the small amount of money I received from the sale of my childhood home and the money he had in his bank account (all split evenly among my siblings), I quit my job at the advertising agency and took a month-long trip through Europe. I had an amazing time and relished in the fact that I was spending his money, some of which was earned by selling marijuana and crystal meth. Yes, my father was also a drug dealer.

In my mid-twenties, I began to experience what I refer to as a somacultural crisis (Johnson, 2018) and began a quest to answer a question that I had ruminated on for many years: "What does love look like?" This question was important because rarely did I find cultural references that included people, characters, or scenarios that looked like ones I was experiencing. Throughout my life I was always able to find cultural references about love (or at least what I thought was love) that mirrored my Euro-American culture, though this was arguably limited in terms of queer and gay perspectives. Finding cultural references to Native American love, let alone Native American Two-Spirit or gay love, was nearly impossible (Alexie, 2002; Bezucha, 2000), and biracial/bicultural expressions of Native Americans of European descent were nonexistent. In my mid-twenties the question "What does love look like?" and, more personally, "What might love look like for me?" led me to take a yearlong sabbatical from dating or sexual intimacy with others to understand what it meant to love myself, which included learning to love my body. During this time, I was introduced to the concept of Two-Spirit people through a friend I had made at the American Indian Community House in New York City. He took me under his wing and shared that we, as Two-Spirit people, were sacred and held special roles in our tribal communities, such as medicine people and land protectors. I met additional people who identified as Two-Spirit and found a community of Native Americans and First Nations people from varying tribal nations who had formed a community of support, companionship, and social justice advocacy.

I was openly embraced and welcomed by the Two-Spirit community and for the first time in my life, felt accepted, and even loved, by a group of people with a shared cultural identity. Coming to understand Two-Spirit and what it means to be Two-Spirit was a catalyst in my life that allowed me to open myself to the possibility of loving myself, my body, my community, and other people. It is through this love, what Muscogee people call *vnokeckv* (community love) that I began to understand that I could decolonize, unsettle, and move closer to my liberation, what I would eventually call somacultural liberation.

I have been married since 2009, when same-sex marriage was only recognized in five states (Connecticut, Iowa, Massachusetts, New Hampshire, and Vermont) and in Washington, DC. My husband identifies as White. Our love has deepened my life in ways that I did not know were possible. Through my own pursuit of questioning "What does love look like?" I have come to believe that love—whether that love is seen through the Western lenses of eros, philia, or agape, or through Indigenous understandings of love—has been the greatest catalyst for growth and liberation in my life. I aspire to help others discover love within their lives as well.

I am approaching my writing through the lens of decolonizing sexuality (Jolivétte, 2016; Morgensen, 2015) and liberation psychology (Martin-Baró, 1994; Watkins & Shulman, 2010). I advocate for a Two-Spirit somacultural liberation, one rooted in resiliency, erotic survivance, and sexual sovereignty. My interest in working doing research with Two-Spirit community has been ongoing since my undergraduate training in anthropology. While completing my graduate degree in counseling psychology, I began working with the Two-Spirit community in the Bay Area by taking on a leadership role. I would eventually be invited to serve as the chair of the board for the Bay Area American Indian Two-Spirits (BAAITS) and eventually the chair of the BAAITS Two-Spirit Powwow in 2020. Having been involved with BAAITS as both a community member and board member has allowed me to foster relationships with other Two-Spirit people and organizations across the United States and Canada. I regard myself as a member of the Two-Spirit community and identify as Two-Spirit. My work within the Two-Spirit community is reflective of roles Two-Spirit people have played and continue to play in tribal communities. Being in service with and for Two-Spirit people continues to be an ongoing value of mine.

I now understand the way I see and make sense of the world around me is through a Two-Spirit lens. With all the multiplicities of my identity, Two-Spirit is the one I most identify with. A portion of this book is dedicated to sharing more about Two-Spirit people and ideologies. Although I do not consider this book to be about Two-Spirit people and ideologies, I believe, because of my identity, this is a Two-Spirit book. I recognize that many people reading this may not know about or have heard about Two-Spirit people. I also recognize people familiar with my work around decolonizing sexuality may want to understand more about the concept of Two-Spirit. I share all of this with you to be reflexive of what Takacs (2003) describes as how our positionality biases our epistemology. The more I claim and write from my Two-Spirit perspective, the closer I am to my liberation. I believe the more you claim all the parts of yourself that make you you, the closer to your liberation you can get. Let us journey together.

5

WHAT IS TWO-SPIRIT?

Cortez, CO, is a popular tourist destination due to its proximity to the Mesa Verde National Park and the Four Corners region, where Colorado, Utah, New Mexico, and Arizona meet. Forty miles southwest of Cortez lies the Navajo Nation, whose tribal territories are home to approximately three hundred thousand Native Americans (US Department of the Interior, 2014, p. 26). The Navajo Nation reservation is also the former home of Fred Martinez Jr., whose body was found outside of Cortez on June 23, 2001 (Hauff, 2019). Martinez was only sixteen when he was bludgeoned to death in an apparent homophobic, transphobic, and racist attack. Martinez had been open to his mother about his sexuality most of his life, and while Fred still struggled with issues of acceptance and nonconformity, Navajo language and tradition helped Fred understand there was a place in the world for someone who encompasses more than one gender, *nádleehí* (Epple, 1998; Nibley, 2009). Martinez's mother shared this word and tradition with her son, enabling Fred to find comfort in the historical traditions of his tribal nation. Director Lydia Nibley documented Fred's short life in the film *Two Spirits* (2009). The film focuses on Martinez's murder and his mother's grief and also further investigates gender and sexuality in Native American communities.

When news spread of Martinez's murder, comparisons began to be made between him and Matthew Shepard. Shepard's body was found outside of Laramie, WY, on October 22, 1998. Matthew died from blunt trauma to the head; he was twenty-one. When Matthew's body was found, he was so disfigured that he was originally mistaken for a scarecrow. Martinez and Shepard shared more than their proximity in age and cause of death: they also identified as gay, and their deaths were the result of homophobic acts perpetrated against them.

The traumatic murders of Fred Martinez Jr. and Matthew Shepard brought national and international attention to the continued struggles and potential dangers for gay, lesbian, bisexual, transgender, and Two-Spirit people living in the United States. Their deaths are also part of a larger collective of cultural trauma, defined as a traumatic event experienced by a group or community either directly or indirectly, which leaves a mark on their consciousness. Shepard's unfortunate death was instrumental in creating The Matthew Shepard and James Byrd, Jr. Hate Crimes Prevention Act, commonly referred to as The Matthew Shepard Act, signed into law by President Barack Obama in 2009. The Matthew Shepard Act created a new federal criminal law that criminalizes willfully causing (or the attempt of) bodily harm when

> *(1) the crime was committed because of the actual or perceived race, color, religion, national origin of any person or (2) the crime was committed because of the actual or perceived religion, national origin, gender, sexual orientation, gender identity, or disability of any person and the crime affected interstate or foreign commerce or occurred within federal special maritime and territorial jurisdiction. (US Department of Justice, n.d.)*

Like Martinez, Matthew Shepard was also out to his family, and similarly, his death was also the subject of media attention including the stage play *The Laramie Project* (2001), which was later made into an HBO feature film, the films *The Matthew Shepard Story* (2002) and *Anatomy of a Hate Crime* (2001), and the documentary *Laramie Inside Out* (2004). Several books, poems, songs, and albums have also been dedicated to Shepard's honor. Matthew Shepard's murder received the most extensive media coverage of several shockingly brutal hate-based murders that made national news during a year's time, and *The Advocate*, a national gay and lesbian news magazine, called the media coverage of the crime an "unprecedented and sympathetic press response" (Noelle, 2002, p. 31). Shepard also appeared on the covers of *Time* and the *New York Times* (NYT). Although Shepard's murder was reported by NYT (no coverage of the Martinez murder appeared in that paper), it took the news agency three days to report on his death. When the newspaper began to focus on the Shepard case, it focused almost exclusively on two elements, the deplorable motives of the perpetrators and the gruesome character of the scene. The headline of the NYT article, "Gay Man Beaten and Left for Dead; 2 Are Charged," speaks to how his murder was sensationalized because of his sexuality, despite Laramie Police Commander O'Malley's public claim at the time that the chief motive of the crime was robbery (Ott & Aoki, 2002, p. 487).

Although various media forums have covered both Martinez and Shepard's deaths, Shepard's death appears to have had a larger impact on society. A simple Google search for Matthew Shepard pulls up approximately ten million web pages, whereas the same search for Fred Martinez Jr. pulls up approximately two million pages. Does race matter when media outlets cover horrific and/or traumatic events? Further, does the lack of media coverage of traumatic events in minority communities perpetuate intergenerational trauma and lead minority groups to further believe their stories do not matter?

Peter Levine (2008) states "trauma is trauma, no matter what caused it" (p. 14). Although Levine's statement may be true in many respects, how is the lens of "trauma is trauma" shifted when we begin to explore how trauma impacts culture? Trauma is both an individual and collective psychological phenomena that has the power to impact past, current, and future generations. A splitting also occurs in collective dynamics of trauma, "when one part of society suffers the atrocity, and another part of society declares that it is time to move on. Often the dominant group, or the group with the most social power, will not include the traumatic story of an oppressed minority group into its collective narrative of events" (Audergon, 2004, p. 21). When discussing the murders of Martinez and Shepard through the lens of collective trauma, it is critical to reassess the impact that colonization has had, not only on Native communities, but also how a colonizing mentality continues to play a role in the politics of the United States policy, education system, media, and social framework.

When reviewing how the national media handled the Matthew Shepard case, Brian L. Ott and Eric Aoki (2002) revealed

> *The news media's tragic framing of the event works rhetorically and ideologically to relieve the public of its social complicity and culpability; to reaffirm a dominant set of discourses that socially stigmatizes gay, lesbian, bisexual, and transgendered (GLBT) persons; and to hamper efforts to create and enact a progressive GLBT social policy. (p. 485)*

One way to look at how the traumatic deaths of Martinez and Shepard have been portrayed in various media outlets is to note the usage of *frame analysis*, which refers to how a traumatic event is defined, and how that definition then shapes public opinion. Frame analysis looks at the inherent biases in all media stories by looking at what is included and excluded in a story, what is emphasized and downplayed, and how the story is structured (Ott & Aoki, 2002). Both the Martinez and Shepard stories have focused on their homosexuality and the fact that heterosexual men killed them. Their stories were also sensationalized when the media depicted the graphic nature of their deaths. What is often left out in Martinez's story by mainstream media are his Navajo culture and the rich tradition of nádleehí, whereas Native media outlets widely report on his Two-Spirit identity.

What makes the gap in culture so evident in these cases? Does it relate to Gabriel Estrada's (2011) concept of a false racialized dichotomy wherein Natives are emotional and spiritual while Euro-Americans are factual and political? Or, is it further evidence of the continued struggle that the approximate ten million American Indian and Alaskan Natives (representing 574 federally recognized tribal nations and 63 state-recognized tribes) living in the United States deal with on an ongoing basis through continued social and historical oppression and intergenerational trauma?

Gender and sexual orientation–based violence at the hands of colonizers has been a lived experience for the Indigenous people of the North American continent since the invasion of 1492. Ethnographic literature dating back to the sixteenth century exemplifies how an ethnocentric ideology on gender and sexual orientation created a deleterious misunderstanding of Indigenous sexuality (Roscoe, 1987). Colonial narratives expressed violent acts being perpetuated on gender- and sexual orientation–variant Indigenous people and eventually a generalized label, berdache,* was applied to Indigenous people who did not fit the European idea of human sexuality (Trexler, 1997). The term *berdache*, used throughout anthropological and ethnographic literature, has been translated as "male sexual slave" (Garrett & Barret, 2003). The term *Two-Spirit* arose to counter this derogatory term and the ethnocentric gender bias of Western colonization.

Native sexuality and sexual practices have been documented since colonization of the Americas. For centuries anthropologists and scholars have been using the term berdache as a blanket term to describe hermaphrodism, transvestitism, and homosexuality in Native American communities, even though there are more than 160 Indigenous North American languages that have words to represent Native people from their cultural perspective. Through the late 1980s, the North American berdache was defined as an Indigenous person, usually male, who was anatomically normal, but assumed the dress, occupation, and behavior of the opposite sex to effect a change in gender (Callender & Kochems, 1983). In 1986, Walter L. Williams's *The Spirit and the Flesh* defined the berdache as a "morphological male who does not fill a society's standard man's role, (one) who has a nonmasculine character . . . androgynous" (p. 2).

An etymological investigation traces the roots of this word:

> *the English word "berdache," or "berdash," indicates that it derived from the French word "bardash," which derived from the Italian word "berdascia," which derived from the Arabic "bardaj," which derived from the Persian "barah." (Angelino & Shedd, 1955, p. 121)*

Europeans appropriated the word during the Crusades and its pronunciation and spelling changed slightly to evolve into its current state. In the 1600s the French began utilizing the term to describe someone engaged in receptive anal sex (Garrett et al., 2003, p. 133). As a term to describe Native Americans who did not fit the Cartesian thought model of dichotomous categorizations, berdache first appeared in colonial ethnographic

* The term berdache was first used by French colonists in the early seventeenth century to describe Native Americans who did not fit the strict gender and sexual orientation roles favored by the European colonizers (Trexler, 2002).

literature in the later part of the sixteenth century (Trexler, 2002, p. 615). From the time of the first contact with Europeans, gender diversity and same-sex relations in Native communities were repressed by religious condemnation and violence of the colonizers. But early accounts that describe the status of berdache as scorned in their communities appear to be more an expression of the European reaction than actual Native views.

I first heard this term in New York City in the early 2000s. I was attending a house party of a friend who lived in Brooklyn and was approached by a man named Ed whom I had met several times prior. He smelled of cigarettes and alcohol and encroached upon my personal space while he was talking to me. I was literally backed into a corner. Ed really wanted to know my racial background. In what has become a typical experience in my life, our conversation went a bit like this.

Ed: So what are you anyway?

Roger: Excuse me? What am I?

Ed: Your race, what's your background. You're so exotic looking.

Roger: Oh, um, thank you, I guess? My mother is Native American, Poarch Creek, and my father is White.

Ed: Oh, so you're a berdache!

Roger: A what?

Ed: It just means that you are a gay Indian.

There was a term for a gay Native person? Wow, I had never heard that before. I thanked Ed for sharing the information with me and squeezed past him. I decided to leave the party so I could go home and do some research on this new term, hoping it would lead me to a deeper understanding of the intersections of my identity. I was living in Spanish Harlem in Manhattan at the time and the train ride from the Park Slope neighborhood in Brooklyn took about an hour. I kept thinking about the word berdache. The word sounded French to me; I had studied French in high school and was a decent-enough French language speaker. When

I arrived home, I sat in front of my computer and waited for the dial-up modem to come online. This was in the days before Google became ubiquitous, so I believe I may have used either the Yahoo search engine or one called HotBot. I typed what I believed would be the spelling of the word (based on my knowledge of the French language) and hit Enter. In a matter of moments, I was offered a few different sites to review. It took me less than 3 minutes to learn that berdache was actually a pejorative that meant "kept boy" or "sexual slave" (according to the site I found). I immediately thought of Ed and our conversation. I wondered if Ed knew that berdache meant that I was more than a "gay Indian." I wondered if he knew and just didn't care because as a White gay male, he didn't have to.

I have heard and received ignorant and racist comments by White gay men so many times that I have lost count. The question of how much Native American you are is an inherently racist one that seeks to delegitimize mixed-race Native people, and many of the White gay men I have experienced in my life really want to know the answer to this question. After learning about the term berdache, I felt even more conflicted about my identity. Now I knew there was a term used to describe someone like me, though its meaning was hurtful. I believe that using this term to refer to Native people who experience sexual orientation and gender variance is the equivalent to calling someone the "f" word or "queer" with a negative connotation.

As an activist, scholar, and therapist in the field of sexuality, I find it ironic that I must engage with the words of the colonizer and explain what makes the terminology not appropriate to use with gender- and sexual orientation–variant Native people. Harjo (2010) explains "the people being colonized are stripped of their names and called belittling ones, often in the language of the colonizer or the enemy of the colonized" (p. 31). I do not have the luxury of not writing about the term berdache. Failing to include the history of colonization and sexuality would negate a crucial understanding of sexuality from Indigenous perspectives. Liberation requires a reckoning with the harms of the past and present.

Katz (1976) examined "448 years of testimony from military men, missionaries, explorers, trappers, traders, settlers, medical doctors, anthropologists, homosexual emancipationists and Gay Indians" (p. 281) and states, "the berdache phenomenon may well have less to do with its incidence than with the fascination of heterosexual observers and their lack of knowledge of less immediately obvious types of Native homosexuality" (p. 282). Famed anthropologist Margaret Mead (1949) wrote this of berdache: "among many American Indian tribes, the berdache, the man who dressed and lived as a woman, is a recognized social institution, counterpointed to the excessive emphasis upon bravery, and hardiness for men" (p. 129). Brown (1997) states, "the word most frequently used, berdache, has a pejorative meaning (sodomite) and seems inappropriate to use" (p. 13). In the five centuries since the colonial exploitation of Native sexuality, berdache has been the commonly held label describing gender and sexual orientation in Native American tribal nations. In an article for the *Journal of Homosexuality*, Roscoe (1987) documented over 137 North American tribal nations who have a word in their Indigenous language for what the colonists named berdache. His bibliography would appear again in *Living the Spirit: A Gay American Indian Anthology* (1988). In the preface to *Living the Spirit* Randy Burns (Northern Paiute) wrote that berdache played important roles in their community including as "artists, providers, and healers"(p. 1). According to Burns, "gay and lesbian American Indians today represent the continuity of these tradition[s]. We are living in the spirit of our gay Indian ancestors" (p. 2). The word berdache is used throughout *Living the Spirit*.

Further academic discourse on berdache can be found in the works of Williams (1986), Roscoe (1988, 1991, 1998), and Herdt (1994). Although these texts use this derogatory term, they remain an important and integral part of the discourse of Indigenous sexuality in North America. Roscoe has had several books published on the subject of gender in Native North America, including *The Zuni Man-Woman* (1991), which examines the life of We'wha, a "berdache," who served as a cultural ambassador of the Zunis and traveled to Washington, DC, in 1886 to "meet national leaders and shake hands with the president" (Roscoe, 1991, p. 2). Roscoe (1991) is mindful that berdache is the "currently accepted anthropological term" and "variations of berdache were once current in Spanish, French, English, and Italian" (p. 5). Roscoe (1988) notes that *gay* is the preferred term over *berdache* for GAI yet also advocates for "berdache studies as a new focus within anthropology as well as American Indian and multidisciplinary gender studies" (p. 82).

I felt haunted by this word and eventually wrote a song called "Two Nations" that exemplifies my struggles with my biracial and bicultural identity. A line from the song states, "So tell me, what do you see? Brown or White? Or do you see the berdache in me?" (2006). When I perform the song live, I always put a strong emphasis on the word. The lyric is meant to be a pushback against all the Eds in the world and people like him whose ignorance around colonial language and Native culture harms Indigenous people.

In *Spaces between Us: Queer Settler Colonialism and Indigenous Decolonization* (2011), Scott Lauria Morgensen explains, "the heteronormativity of settler colonialism has subjected Native and non-Native people to settler colonial rule and regimes of modern sexuality" (p. 2). Making sexuality and gender diversity a central reason to justify the conquest of North America, the effort to civilize Native Americans, and the consequent disavowal of Indigenous traditions can be understood as significantly contributing to the institutionalization of heteronormative standards and behavior in Native communities because "U.S. imperialism against Native peoples over the past two centuries can be understood as an effort to make them straight and insert Indigenous peoples into Anglo-American conceptions of family, home, desire, and personal identity" (Rifkin, 2011b, p. 8). It is necessary to understand the long-lasting effects of colonization on Native people to recognize the burden of inequality that is felt in the lives of Two-Sprit people today.

As an act of decolonization against berdache and as a claim for sexual sovereignty, a group of Native American and First Nations activists came together in community near Winnipeg, Canada, in 1990. Participants at the Winnipeg gathering chose the term *Two-Spirit*, defined as "the presence of both the masculine and the feminine spirit in one person, Two-Spirit in English referred at once to gay, lesbian, transgender, as well as wintke, nádleehi, and other appropriate tribal terms" (Morgensen, 2011, p. 81). The gathering in Winnipeg and the proclamation of Two-Spirit inspired the writings of Driskill (2011a, 2011b), Finley (2011), Gilley (2006, 2011), Morgensen (2011, 2015), Jolivétte (2016), Vernon (2001), Rifkin (2011a,

2011b), Tatonetti (2014), whose combined work focuses on traditional and contemporary roles Two-Spirit people contribute to Native life. Further, their work takes a decolonized approach to Two-Spirit and 2SLGBTQIA+ sexuality.

The term Two-Spirit was proposed by Myra Laramee (Fisher River Cree) and unanimously accepted to be inclusive of Indigenous people who identify as lesbian, gay, bisexual, transgender, or queer, or through nationally specific terms from Indigenous languages. Two-Spirit was derived from the Northern Algonquin phrase *niizh manitoag*, meaning "two-spirits" (Balsam et al., 2004). The term Two-Spirit allowed individuals who were living within the cultural and social sphere of their tribal communities to bring together their sexual orientation and their Native identity. The importance of the adopted terminology is perhaps best summed up by cofounder of the Minnesota Two-Spirit Society, Richard La Fortune (Yupik), who stated, "we are remembering who we are, and that our identities cannot be used as weapons against us" (Morgensen, 2011, p. 24).

In the earlier anthropological record regarding Native people, there is conflicting discourse regarding sex and gender. It is important to note that "when we connect sex and gender, we are not comparing something social with something natural, rather we are comparing something social with something that is also social" (Goulet, 1996, p. 686). Two-Spirit identity is not a form of institutionalized homosexuality that can be compared to a Eurocentric placation on same-sex practices. Discussions most often proceed without referencing Indigenous conceptualizations of the body, but without these conversations, a key element to the uniqueness of Two-Spirit identity is missing.

The use of the term Two-Spirit is also an example of shifts in decolonial discourse to be more inclusive of people in addition to land. Tuck and Yang (2012) assert that "within settler colonialism, the most important concern is land/water/air/subterranean earth. Land is what is most valuable, contested, required" (p. 5). If decolonial discourse was more inclusive of not just land, but also the bodies on land (which includes 2SLGBTQIA+ Indigenous people), perhaps gender- and sexual orientation–based violence, like that experienced by Fred Martinez Jr., would be less, not just for Indigenous people, but for all BIPOC people. Without the inclusion of sexuality (including gender and sexuality), decolonial discourse is limited to Indigenous bodies whose sexuality already mirrors the oppressors (Simpson, 2017). This reductive imposition threatens sovereignty because it erases Indigenous agency over 2SLGBTQIA+ Indigenous bodies.

The exclusion of Two-Spirit voices and bodies perpetuates colonial ideologies that have worked to erase queerness from Indigeneity and normalize gender- and sexual orientation–based violence. The story of Fred Martinez Jr. is, tragically, not unique. Violence against queer Indigenous people has been a tool of colonial domination since the Iberian invasion of the lands we now call Mexico and Central America (Trexler, 1997), as well as the invasion of the rest of Turtle Island, now referred to as North America (Finley, 2011). Sexuality became an additional frontier that was subjected to heteropatriarchal perspectives, erasing the Indigeneity of queerness in the peoples and culture through invasion and seizure of land.

The erasure of queerness in Native communities also created an erasure of Native queerness in 2SLGBTQIA+ spaces and communities (Katz, 1976). The term Two-Spirit is an example of this erasure, as it was coined to push back against colonial terminology that was used by settlers to describe gender and sexual orientation variance in Indigenous people. Two-Spirit became a term many Native queer and 2SLGBTQIA+ people and allies could get behind because it used imposed colonial language and reclaimed Indigenous identity and survivance (Vizenor, 2008). Two-Spirit shifted the narrative from erasure to equity and equal representation.

Yet, for Two-Spirit people, the impact of exclusion is ongoing and is evidenced by challenges to education and preventative treatments regarding sexual health, especially around HIV/AIDS (Jolivétte, 2016). Not only have Native Americans often been misidentified or not included in racial demographics in HIV/AIDS research, but the absence of culturally aware interventions for HIV/AIDS has imparted an additional colonial trauma upon Native American and Two-Spirit people. Without proper support from Indian Health Services and the larger 2SLGBTQIA+ community, the sexual health needs of Two-Spirit people are left unheard and therefore unfulfilled.

The attempted erasure of gender and sexual orientation variance in Native people is an example of what has been defined as *postcolonial violence* (the ongoing settler violence that continues to be perpetuated on Two-Spirit people). The general problem is this type of violence is perpetuated by excluding and attempting to erase gender- and sexual orientation–variant Indigenous people. According to Trask (2004),

> *In a colonial country such as the United States, white hegemony delineates white people are the dominant group, Christianity is the dominant religion, capitalism is the dominant economy, and militarism is the dominant form of diplomacy and the underlying force of international relations. Violence is thus normal, and race prejudice, like race violence, is as American as apple pie (p. 10).*

Trask's perspective defines postcolonial violence for what it is, an examination of "colonizer–colonized binaries" (Hartmann, Wendt, Burrage, Pomerville, & Gone, 2019, p. 4). These binaries are not exclusive to Two-Spirit, American Indian/Alaska Native, or First Nations people; rather numerous examples of postcolonial violence relating to race-based gender and sexual orientation can be found throughout history (Bakshi, Jivraj, & Posocco, 2016; Collins, 2005). The most prominent of these is perhaps the example of Black people of all genders who continue to be eroticized and subjected to identity tropes that perpetuate harmful stereotypes and sexual violence (Taylor, 2018).

Indigenous people are perpetually reminded of postcolonial violence by the settler state's ongoing efforts to create laws that break treaties, endanger sacred sites, destroy environmental resources such as fresh water, and limit access to land. American Indians only gained the legal right to practice what was deemed "religion" in 1978. The American Indian Religious Freedom Act (AIRFA) of 1978 (42 U.S.C. § 1996) "protects the rights of Native Americans to exercise their traditional religions by ensuring access to sites, use and possession of sacred objects, and the freedom to worship through ceremonials and traditional rites" (National Oceanic and Atmospheric Administration, Office for Coastal Management, n.d., p. 1). One defining aspect of Two-Spirit identity is a connection to spiritual traditions, practices, and ideologies. The recurrent violence experienced by Two-Spirit people is in direct violation of AIRFA and must be included in further advocacy for Two-Spirit people.

Gender- and sexual orientation–variant Indigenous people face the continual threat of erasure because they are often not acknowledged, included, or represented in numerous areas of public life including the sexual health and wellness healthcare sphere. Since the 1980s one of the most profound realities of exclusion and postcolonial violence is indicated by the United States government's response to the HIV/AIDS pandemic for Native people, which includes 2SLGBTQIA+ Natives (Jolivétte, 2016; Vernon, 2001). The government's response highlights continual misrepresentation and misunderstandings by non-Native, non-Two-Spirit, non-LGBTQIA+ people in positions of power. This is further evidenced by LGBTQIA+ communities not offering Indigenous gender- and sexual orientation–variant people representation regarding issues pertaining to them. A recent trend of many festivals and conferences has been to ask Indigenous people to offer an opening blessing as well as a land acknowledgment, and then to escort the Indigenous person or group from said activity and not include them in any further discussions. This erasure perpetuates the colonial ideology that Indigenous people are props for spiritual bypassing; their role is to ease the guilt and shame of the dominant White LGBTQIA+ and settler community. Further, gender- and sexual orientation–variant Indigenous people face erasure by LGBTQIA+ communities through the perpetuation of sexual tropes against Indigenous people and bodies, including non-Indigenous people co-opting the term Two-Spirit, wearing traditional regalia, or holding and participating in traditional ceremonies.

Regarding Two-Spirit people, the works of Katz (1976), Williams (1986), and Roscoe (1987) are resources that create syntax to explore themes of gender and sexual orientation pre- and post-contact with Westerners, yet these do not explicitly relate to Native LGBTQIA+ and/or Two-Spirit love, pleasure, and sexual subjectivity. Contemporary works by Morgensen (2011), Rifkin (2011b), and Jolivétte (2016) help Native LGBTQIA+ and/or Two-Spirit people understand the implications of colonization on gender and sexuality in Indian country, yet they also remain elusive about love and pleasure. These works, which are important works in queer and

Native studies, not only provide a thorough historical analysis, but also a contemporary focus on decolonization. To include love, sensuality, and pleasure in the Two-Spirit discourse is to animate the Two-Spirit subjective perspective and thus claim sexual sovereignty. Claiming sexual sovereignty directly challenges patriarchal power structures, which continue to perpetuate detrimental narratives about Two-Spirit people and to ignore important aspects of the experience of its peoples.

Decolonizing sexuality is a multitiered process of challenging dominant narratives of sexuality to advocate for sexual sovereignty and erotic survivance. Decolonizing sexuality is not limited to an academic discourse. Rather, it is an engaged process that includes the emotional, somatic, spiritual, and sexual experiences that all colonized, oppressed, and marginalized people have a right to explore and claim as part of their sovereignty and lived bodily experiences. Decolonizing sexuality means dismantling exploitative practices, policies, discourse, and culture that subjugate and colonize the sexuality of Indigenous people, including those who identify as 2SLGBTQIA+. Rifkin (2011a) adds to the discourse by stating, "decolonization partially entails a changed understanding of the relation between sexuality and sovereignty, in which the former does not serve as a basis for exiling people from inclusion in the latter" (p. 174). For this changed understanding to disseminate across tribal nations, the process of decolonizing sexuality must not be limited to the individual; it needs to include tribal communities, tribal nations, and tribal leadership. It is imperative to also include working and partnering with allies, and changing the cultural landscape we are currently traversing. The process of decolonization is not limited only to land. Additionally, we must evaluate it from multiple perspectives in which Indigenous people have been impacted by colonization, including critically examining sexual sovereignty and the concepts of gender and sexual orientation as they apply to Native American and First Nations people before first contact with Europeans.

Situating sexuality from the perspective of sovereignty encompasses what Andrea Smith (2011) calls "unsettling settler colonialism" (p. 43). Settler colonialism and the projection of Eurocentric values on Indigenous sexuality led to the systemic eradication of sexual sovereignty. Decolonization, including decolonizing sexuality, is a process of reclamation wherein those who have survived genocide engage in ceremony and advocate for social and sexual justice issues, which uplift Indigenous people and serve as a part of the healing process. According to Linda Smith (1999),

> *Decolonization . . . does not mean and has not meant a total rejection of all theory or research or Western knowledge. Rather, it is about centering our concerns and world views and then coming to know and understand theory and research from our own perspectives and for our own purposes. (p. 39)*

A part of the knowing and the understanding Smith advocates for must be inclusive of diverse perspectives on gender and sexuality in North America pre- and post-contact. Roscoe (1998) states,

> *When it comes to the history of Native Americans, we can no longer cling to a pre-Foucauldian idea of power flowing in only one direction and always from the top down, for we will invariably end up characterizing American Indians as passive recipients of White conquest and culture. (p. 218)*

Foucault's (1978) idea of power and sex are relevant because he believes "to say that sex is not repressed, or rather that the relationship between sex and power is not characterized by repression, is to risk falling into a sterile paradox" (p. 117). Not including sexuality in the discussion around decolonization would result in a similar sterile paradox and perpetuate the exotification and objectification and thus colonization of Native desire.

It is important to situate sexuality (which includes gender, sexual orientation, sexual behaviors, sexual health, and vitality, as well as culture) as part of the conversation when discussing colonization. Jolivétte (2016) postulates, "unpacking relationships between Indigenous, colonizing, and other marginalized populations is central to the project of decolonizing gender, sexuality, and mixed-race identity(ies) within Native communities and nations as well as from among the rest of U.S. society" (p. 81).

Terms such as *berdache* and *Two-Spirit* exist as a counterpoint to perceptions of normative gender and/or sexual orientation behavior favored by Europeans, whereas the terms *heterosexuality* and *homosexuality* were not introduced into the lexicon until 1868 (Katz, Duggan, & Vidal, 1995, p. 52). Brown (1997) states gay American Indians "endure the oppression of their sexuality but also the minority status of Indians, while lesbians must also endure the oppression of their female gender" (p. xxi). The term Two-Spirit, though sometimes used as an umbrella term for those who may identify as LGBTQIA+ and also identify as Native American/American Indian/Indian/First Nations/Aboriginal, is not meant as a replacement for Indigenous languages that already have a word to describe Two-Spirit people. Examples include *wintke* (Dakota), *nádleehi* (Navajo), *lhamana* (Zuni), and *ennvrkvpv* (Creek) (Roscoe, 1987). Gilley (2006) notes that in "American Indian studies, and gay Native social circles, Two-Spirit essentially refers to a personal subjectivity consisting of two spirits, one male and one female" (p. 127). Debate within the Two-Spirit community continues as to the definition of Two-Spirit and the role Two-Spirit people should take in social justice movements.

Two-Spirit encompasses both gender and sexual orientation. Some scholars (e.g., Roscoe, 1998; Williams, 1986) focus on the gender aspect of Two-Spirit, whereas Jolivétte (2016) focuses on gender and sexual orientation. In terms of Two-Spirit and gender, Butler's (1990) concept of *performativity* can be used as an exploration of the performance of Two-Spirit identity. In Butler's theory, in order for something to be performative, it must produce a series of results. According to Butler, "the view that gender is performative sought to show that what we take to be an internal essence of gender is manufactured through a sustained set of acts" (p. 195). Two-Spirit exemplifies the concept of performativity because it produces an extension of cultural practices that were present before and after colonization. These cultural practices produce(d) a connection to community, spirit, and sexual sovereignty. An extension of Butler's theory can be found in the work of Innes and Anderson (2015) who posit, "the performance of Indigenous masculinity has been profoundly impacted by colonization and the imposition of a White supremacist, heteronormative patriarchy that has left a lasting and negative legacy for Indigenous women, children, elders, and their communities as a whole" (p. 4). Two-Spirit (inclusive of all gender expressions) is performed through engagement with self as a reflexive inquiry and then extended to community inclusive of Native American and First Nations people. Two-Spirit is also an identity for Native American and First Nations people to use as best resonates with them.

Where and how do LGBTQIA+ Natives and/or Two-Spirit people learn about sexual and sensual pleasure? To include sensuality and pleasure into the Two-Spirit discourse is to claim sexual sovereignty. Claiming sexual sovereignty directly challenges patriarchal power structures that continue to perpetuate deleterious narratives about Two-Spirit people. Without the inclusion of sensuality and pleasure, Two-Spirit people are relegated to a mythical status of pan-shaman.

Organizations such as the Bay Area American Indian Two-Spirits (BAAITS), the Montana Two Spirit Society (MTSS), the East Coast Two Spirit Society (EC2SS), as well as the International Council of Two Spirit Societies, are representations of Two-Spirit love in action because of their communal work to ensure Two-Spirit people have access to their culture, as well as preventative health, including HIV/AIDS awareness and treatment, and inclusion in sacred ceremonies in their home-based and pan-tribal communities. The shared identities Two-Spirit communities have (which include sexuality, race and ethnicity, colonization, homophobia, genderphobia) create a sense of communion with others that goes beyond mere cooperation. These shared identities offer Two-Spirit people a place for fellowship and companionship and an opportunity to participate in or learn ceremonial roles and activities they may have been excluded from in their tribal communities due to homophobic and gender phobic biases brought by colonization. Two-Spirit communities are not unique in their representation of philia in action and they are not immune to the foibles that can, at times, belie any community or organization. Yet it is a shared ambition of returning to the circle, a practice that conjures healing through traditional ways and that distinguishes the Two-Spirit community as its own unique example of philia.

While I was doing research for my dissertation, I had an opportunity to chat with Gay American Indians (GAI) cofounder Randy Burns about the work that he has done in the Two-Spirit community. He expressed that current Two-Spirit scholarship focuses primarily on urban-based people, which brings an urban perspective. When I asked Burns about the importance of Two-Spirit voices being a part of the discourse around Indigenous sexuality, Burns had this to say: "Native American people can speak for themselves." Burns described his childhood growing up in northern

Nevada as an isolating experience, where he wondered if there were others like him in the world. He shared that his experience as a reservation and rural Native person meant that the expression of his sexuality and his gay identity were often confined to spaces deemed dirty by society (such as truck stops and cruising zones). When asked about berdache, Burns shared that when he first learned of the word, it was not considered a pejorative, and that many gay American Indians were thankful for a pan-tribal term that would bring them together. Burns also spoke of the necessity for historical trauma to be a continued piece of the dialogue around Two-Spirit people. Since GAI was the first pan-Native LGBTQIA+ organization, it is often seen as an inspiration for the creation of other 2SLGBTQIA+ organizations across the United States and Canada. Currently, sixteen Two-Spirit societies from North America have come together to form the International Counsel of Two-Spirit Societies (ICTS). One of the goals of ICTS is to foster communication around issues impacting Two-Spirit people including sexual vitality, health and wellness, HIV/AIDS, language preservation, cultural restoration, and advocating for the inclusion of 2SLGBTQIA+ Natives in ceremony and ritual in Native communities.

TWO-SPIRIT IDENTITY

Two-Spirit as an identity is rich and complex. The term was first coined in 1990 (Morgensen, 2011) challenging years of problematic language perpetuated by anthropologists (Mead, 1949; Roscoe, 1987). It is first and foremost situated within Indigeneity, and though the term has been culturally appropriated by people and groups who are not Indigenous, it is imperative you understand the term Two-Spirit is political. This is because claiming Indigenous blood, land, and tribal enrollment is a political act in and of itself due to the blood quotient requirements of the Bureau of Indian Affairs (United States) and Indigenous and Northern Affairs Canada that force members of sovereign nations to prove they are Indigenous. No other racial group in the United States or Canada is required to prove membership in a racial or ethnic group.

The concept of being Two-Spirit is not directly linked to sex or sexuality, which is why some Native people consider themselves to be both

Two-Spirit and lesbian, gay, bisexual, or transgender and others consider themselves only LGBTQIA+. Two-Spirit identity is linked to both a general orientation and a role that they play within their community, linking gender and sexuality but not forcing them into compartmentalized categories. When we don't discuss sexuality and gender as separate but equal components of Two-Spirit identity, we risk minimizing the important functions both play in Two-Spirit culture.

Indigenous identities can be deeply complex, especially when considering the role blood politics, sovereignty, and enrollment issues can play in Native communities. Two-Spirit identity is defined by qualities beyond sexuality or gender because it embraces more than just gender and sexuality; it embraces the whole spirit. Two-Spirit is also an identity that is used the same way a Native person might use their tribal affiliation to say something about their cultural heritage (i.e., Poarch Creek). Two-Spirit people recognize that their social and spiritual practices, whether with their tribal community or outside of their community in intertribal ritual or community participation, separate them from their sexual identity as LGBTQIA+. They value the importance of "keeping one foot in the gay world, where sexuality is accepted, and one foot in the Indian world where cultural heritage lies" (Gilley, 2006, p. 89). For the Two-Spirit individual today, there is juxtaposition between the desire to be socially LGBTQIA+ to find acceptance and sexual partners, and the desire to be socially, spiritually, and culturally Native.

Two-Spirits differ from LGBTQIA+ because of how they define themselves in terms of spirituality, work, and social roles. Most Two-Spirit people report having childhood proclivities toward social roles differing from their assigned gender at birth and continue these proclivities through adulthood. Two-Spirit identity is one "created by spirit for a specific purpose that will benefit the community" (Prince-Hughes, 1998, p. 33). The usage of Two-Spirit by non-Natives to define a larger majority of gay and lesbian subculture (i.e., Radical Faeries) has offended Native activists who have spoken out against the majority LGBTQIA+ culture by reminding them "the term Two-Spirited has a specific cultural context and removing it from that context simply because one likes the meaning of it is an act of colonization and must be resisted" (Cameron, 2005, p.123).

Although the motives of using the term Two-Spirit by non-Native groups is unknown, a probable cause is the impact colonization has on cultural appropriation.

The politicizing of Two-Spirit identity from a traditional to a contemporary perspective does not leave room for Two-Spirit people who may have been raised outside of their Native communities and culture and therefore did not have the opportunity to participate in ceremonies related to Two-Spirit tradition. The traditional qualifications of Two-Spiritedness also create the potential for further areas of discrimination within the Two-Spirit community by bringing in questions of blood quantum and physical characteristics as identifiers of Native authenticity (i.e., skin color and hair). Native scholar and activist Phillip Deloria's study of "Indian play" states, "the highest possible degree of authenticity [was] inhered in the traditional, reservation-based full blood (and) the least authentic figure was the progressive, urban, low-quantum mixed-blood" (Gilley, 2006, p. 115). While Deloria's claims are felt throughout the Native and non-Native community, perhaps this concept is doubly felt in the Two-Spirit community, whose members are already dealing with a double marginalized status, that of being Native and of being Two-Spirit and/or LGBTQIA+.

Terminology and how words are defined is an increasingly polarizing notion in contemporary Two-Spirit society. For some LGBTQIA+ Natives, *gay* is the preferred descriptive word because of the way they were raised or as a moniker to stand against homophobia. Other Natives prefer the term *Indigiqueer* to fight the binary classification systems of gender and sexual orientation established by colonialism. Still, others prefer the term *Two-Spirit* because it encompasses more than sexuality and gender and places emphasis on Native identity (Epple, 1998, p. 280).

TWO-SPIRIT LOVE

Love is believed to be universal (Hatfield & Rapson, 2005), yet its meaning and expression vary from culture to culture (Fisher, 2005). Countless works of art as well as nonfiction texts have celebrated the joyful and the sometimes-painful associations human beings experience with love. I am interested in love from a cultural and an erotic perspective, and from what Western philosophers refer to as *philia* and what Muscogee people refer to as *vnokeckv*, or community love. My doctoral research and ongoing work in American Indian studies and sexuality studies suggest an examination of the cultural expression of love to build the foundation of Two-Spirit sexual sovereignty and erotic survivance.

Sexual sovereignty is a direct challenge to settler colonialism and heterocentric idealism, which both fail at understanding how Indigenous communities experience gender and sexuality. Sexual sovereignty is also a claim that Two-Spirit bodies have a right to identify with gender and sexual orientation fluidity and the physical acts of intimacy, pleasure, and sex as an extension of decolonization and a return to Indigenous roles, identities, and practices that existed prior to first contact. Erotic survivance is an extension of Gerald Vizenor's (2008) survivance and Brian Gilley's (2011) sexual survivance and creates space for Two-Spirit people to share and express how their sexuality (gender, orientation, practice) has been an important aspect of their story of survival. Further, erotic survivance is the stories, poetry, prose, songs, dances, medicine, and gatherings Two-Spirit people and communities engage in to celebrate their resiliency, survival, sexual expression, and sexual sovereignty. Two-Spirit literature (DinéYazhi, 2015; Roscoe, 1987) exemplifies the survival and resistance (survivance) of Two-Spirit people as well as leaving space for additional questions, such as "What role does love play in Two-Spirit sexual sovereignty and erotic survivance?" This question bears additional weight when we consider the political and social climate of the United States in the year 2023 due to political unrest, social justice activism, and the ongoing Covid-19 pandemic. The sovereignty of Indigenous people, including Two-Spirit people, is at risk. These issues, as well as the epidemic of missing and murdered Indigenous women, including trans and Two-Spirit Indigenous women, further show the necessity of advocating for the inclusion of Two-Spirit people in all areas of discourse.

In addition to my examination of what I call somacultural liberation, I am curious to investigate how Two-Spirit people (some of whom may identify, behave, or relate to others in ways that place them outside the dominant cultural narrative around sexuality and love) experience love, and the potentially related concepts of intimacy, pleasure, and sex. The purpose of focusing on Two-Spirit people, as opposed to other racial and ethnic groups, or other marginalized gender and sexual orientations, is both personal and political. Personal, because I identify as Two-Spirit and have a desire to give back to a community of people who have been instrumental in my development and growth as a leader, scholar, and artist. Political, because as a racial and ethnic identity, Two-Spirit people are forced through the governments of the United States and Canada to prove citizenship with federal- or state-recognized sovereign nations.

One of my favorite artists is the interdisciplinary Cree visual artist Kent Monkman. I enjoy Monkman's work for my own personal gratification, and I also use his work as an example to share the intersections of sexuality, Indigeneity, and art with audiences. In some of his work, Monkman paints and performs as Miss Chief Eagle Testickle. In an interview for The Metropolitan Museum of Art, Monkman stated he created Miss Chief Eagle Testickle to "offer an Indigenous perspective on the European settlers and to also present a very empowered point of view of Indigenous sexuality pre-contact" (2019). My favorite piece of his is titled *Study for Artist and Model*. The painting depicts an inverse of the popular Edward Curtis photography of Native Americans and First Nations people. In *Study for Artist and Model*, Miss Chief Eagle Testickle is in the role of artist with a White settler tied to a tree with arrows sticking out of his body. When I show the painting to people, there is often a mixed reaction of laughter, cheering, utter confusion, and, occasionally, anger. After presenting on the topic of Two-Spirit people for a Human Sexuality course I used to teach (for which I received racist backlash from some of the students), a White cis-straight male approached me. He asked me how he was supposed to feel looking at a painting of a White man tied to a tree with arrows sticking out of his body. I asked him if he would take a closer look at the picture with me and we could have a deeper conversation. He agreed and I asked him to really look at the painting. His eyes widened when he realized the White man tied to the tree had an erection. He started to laugh nervously and said, "Okay, never mind," and started to walk out. Before he left the room, he turned and said, "Sorry I misunderstood."

"What part?" I asked him.

"I think all of it." He gave me a smile, a nod of his head, and left.

For the remainder of the time in the class, he was attentive, he engaged in conversation with me and other students, and he advocated for, several times, the importance of shifting perspectives around sexuality. Had I responded to his initial inquiry from a defensive place, we may have had a very different semester. Instead, approaching him with curiosity, recognizing the cultural conflict, and inviting him into a brief process created a bridge between our worlds.

When I have been confronted about the Monkman piece, I always ask folks to take a deeper look at the painting. What does it mean for Miss Chief to be in control in the situation? What does it mean that a White man is tied to a tree? What does it mean that the man has an erection? What is offensive to you? The inverse of power? The unabashed display of sexuality? The gender identity of Miss Chief? I then ask people what they notice in their body when they look at the painting. I also ask people about the feelings that emerge and any questions the painting or subject matter brings up. I use a somacultural liberatory framework to help me better understand what the person or people may be experiencing and what, if anything, can be done to help them regulate their nervous system. It is never my intention to purposefully shock anyone, nor do I intentionally choose readings, videos, and other forms of media to push buttons. I am not about pushing buttons; I am about listening to the pull of curiosity that resides within. I also do not believe it is on me to rescue someone who may have a challenge with the material I have presented and how I have presented it. I will listen, I will not rescue. I will not apologize for my promotion of Indigenous sexuality. I will not apologize for the criticism I have toward colonialism and ongoing settler rule. I will not apologize for the discomfort you may feel when rectifying your relationship to Indigenous people, specifically Two-Spirit people, and the land that you now occupy. I will stand firm in my convictions. My ancestors have my back. When I refer to ancestors, I am referring to my ancestors from the Muscogee nation as well as my ancestors whom we would now gently wrap under the umbrella of the term Two-Spirit.

In 2006 I was invited to join a group called Amerinda, an organization that promotes and supports Native actors, musicians, dancers, writers, and directors. During one of their community events, I met another Native named Patrick. We became fast friends, and a week or two later, Patrick invited me to what he called a Two-Spirit community meeting. I remember asking Patrick what Two-Spirit meant, and his response was "Oh, Two-Spirit, that's people like you and me." He gave me a smile and a wink and I understood his nonverbal communication to signal that he was referring to our sexuality. Upon attending my first Two-Spirit meeting with the NorthEast Two-Spirit Society, I immediately felt at home. I was so incredibly excited to meet other Native and mixed-race Native people with a shared identity. I had finally found community. A few months after attending my first Two-Spirit community meeting, I was on a plane bound for Oklahoma to attend a Two-Spirit gathering. The gathering lasted three days and was filled with cultural teachings, sexual health information sessions, a talent show, and a powwow. It was blissful. I met a lot of Two-Spirit people and remain friends with all of them to this day. One of the people that I met at the gathering is Miko Thomas, also known by her drag persona Landa Lakes.

Miko and I have been Two-Spirit collaborators for almost two decades. In the summer of 2007, I was one of the organizers of a Two-Spirit variety show hosted by the Fresh Fruit Festival in New York City. Miko was the first person I contacted to see if they were interested and available. She said yes, and since then, we have appeared on stage and in public conversation with one another multiple times. Most recently, Miko and I (along with a group of amazing Two-Spirit people and allies) have been community organizers of the largest Two-Spirit powwow in the world, the Bay Area American Indian Two-Spirits (BAAITS) Powwow, which takes place in San Francisco. The BAAITS Powwow welcomes approximately five thousand people each year and continues to grow. It was a BAAITS Powwow in 2017 that changed the trajectory of my academic life and research.

Powwows open with what is called *grand entry*. During grand entry, powwow attendees who are also veterans of the US armed services enter the arena, a circle space where the dancing and drumming take place.

The veterans are then followed by the dancers who are participating in the powwow. Following the dancers are any community members who want to participate in the grand entry, and finally any allies who want to participate are also welcome. I always try to be a part of grand entry, though on this particular occasion, I was unable to participate because one of the volunteers needed assistance with the area that was designated for dancers to rest, hydrate, and nourish themselves with food. The hospitality lounge was in an elevated loft space in the Fort Mason Center where we held our powwow. I looked out to the crowd and watched the grand entry. As I watched, I began to cry, and smile, and laugh. I felt such an immense feeling of joy. I felt such an immense feeling of community. I felt such an immense feeling of love.

In the Muscogee language, the language of my maternal family, we have a word, *vnokeckv*. This is our word for love, though vnokeckv does not mean love in the romantic sense. Vnokeckv is the word we use to describe community love. While I was watching the grand entry of the BAAITS Powwow, I was struck by the feeling of vnokeckv. It was an incredibly profound moment in my life and was the inspiration for my dissertation research, which resulted in the title of my dissertation: *Two-Spirit Love: Toward an Inclusion of Sexual Sovereignty and Erotic Survivance*. My research focuses on how other Two-Spirit people defined love. During my research I found that the primary expression of Two-Spirit love is community, as all of the informants of my study named community as their definition of Two-Spirit love. My hypothesis was correct, vnokeckv is not just a Muscogee phenomenon; at its core vnokeckv is an Indigenous ideology. Vnokeckv means that I and all Two-Spirit people belong because the idea of community love is embedded within our language and our culture. Our culture is one of love.

Of course I wish it were as easy as that. Due to colonization, forced removal from our ancestral homelands due to the Indian Removal Act of 1830, and forced assimilation to Christianity, which designed gender and sexual orientation variance as sinful, several members of my tribal community are homophobic, including one of my uncles (despite his own child identifying as bisexual). Gender and sexual orientation variance are a fairly common experience in my family and in my larger tribal community. Several of my cousins identify as Two-Spirit and though never fully disclosed to the larger family while he was alive, one of my uncles identified as gay. During a visit to the reservation a few years back I met up with one of my cousins who had dedicated most of his professional life working in service of our tribal community. We talked about life, religion, music, being mixed-race, and also being gay. When talking about our sexuality, he shared the following with me:

Cousin: Did you know there is a word for people like us in Muscogee?

Rog: Wow, no, I did not know that. What is it?

Cousin: Ennvrkvpv (pronounced In-Nuth-Gah-Bah)

Rog: Really, cousin? Ennvrkvpv (I said sarcastically).

Cousin laughing: Yes, cousin, ennvrkvpv.

Rog: So you're telling me the Muscogee word for Two-Spirit is ennvrkvpv? Wednesday?

Cousin: Well, what does Wednesday mean?

Rog: Well it's the middle of the week.

I paused for a moment and reflected on what I had just said. Wednesday is the middle of the week and *ennvrkvpv* means the middle. Two-Spirit is like being in the middle. It felt right to me. It felt powerful to me. I always liked calling myself Two-Spirit over gay, though once I learned that some people in and around the Poarch Creek Indians Reservation as well as some people in and around the Muscogee reservation in Oklahoma were using ennvrkvpv to describe Two-Spirit people, it became my preferred way to identify my sexuality.

I want to clarify that when I say Two-Spirit is like being in the middle, I am not referring to a colonial binary of two genders, or hetero/homosexual. I am referring to the circular nature of life that gender and sexual orientation are a natural part of. Imagine for a moment a sphere floating in the air. In the center of that three-dimensional shape is Two-Spirit. What I appreciate about this perspective is that with my identity as a Two-Spirit person, I can travel along any spectrum of gender and sexual orientation variance that I feel most comfortable with. Imagine a world that existed in a spherical realm instead of the binary that has been normalized and exemplified as the only cultural way to understand sexuality.

Language is a unique marker for culture with words and their definitions varying throughout time, region, and communities. Ennvrkvpv became a way for me to understand my sexuality from a specific cultural lens, one that was unique to me (and other Muscogee people) among other Two-Spirit and/or LGBTQIA+ people. Though Muscogee speakers may have differing opinions as to whether ennvrkvpv was used historically as an identifier for gender and/or sexual orientation variance, it is being used currently, which exemplifies an evolution of language as a living cultural phenomenon.

Language has the power to establish cultural norms. Throughout the history of the United States, words that were once used as pejorative have sometimes been coopted by the community that had historically been targeted with the word. *Queer* is an example of this evolution. During my childhood in the 1980s, I specifically remember being called queer (along with other harsh words used as pejoratives). LGBTQIA+ activists began to use the word as a unifying term and queer is now used as way to identify variance without labeling one's gender or sexual orientation. Some Indigenous communities also use the term Indigiqueer in addition to and/or as a replacement for the term Two-Spirit because Two-Spirit is perpetually coopted by gay White populations. Recently, I was a guest on a nationally syndicated LGBTQIA+ radio program hosted by two White DJs. I was asked if it was okay for non-Native people to use the term Two-Spirit, with one of the hosts saying that she does use the term. My response focused on land theft, culture theft, and displacement. Her male counterpart laughed and told her she had just been canceled. I made a note to never appear on the program again, and if asked, I would tell them I was not interested in promoting ignorant ideologies for a few laughs. Safety is never a laughing matter, and ennvrkvpv has given me a feeling of safety because I feel that I belong.

Though no member of my maternal family has ever been directly homophobic to me, I am aware that members of my immediate family as well as members of my tribal community are homophobic. I have seen social media posts by tribal members ridiculing a gay tribal council member and trying to get him voted off tribal council for attending a drag show. His appearance at a drag show was being used to try and disqualify him from serving our people. Thankfully the homophobic campaign did not yield the result the tribal members had intended.

Since learning about the term Two-Spirit and then later learning about the term ennvrkvpv, I have felt a renewed sense of purpose and identity when I am visiting my family on the Poarch Reservation. Should any tribal member, including tribal members who are family, ever try to impose colonial ideologies onto my sexuality, I will remind them that I am ennvrkvpv and that my sexuality and the expression of my sexuality are sacred. I will remind them they are echoing the violence that murdered thousands of our ancestors and separated our tribal communities so White people could steal our land, enslave Black people, and profit off genocide and forced servitude. I am not afraid to speak what I know is true about the region of the United States from which my tribal community originates and still lives. Without the middle, there is no balance, and the circle of healing will never be complete. Two-Spirit and Indigiqueer people are needed for full balance of our tribal communities and to remind the colonizers and settlers they failed in the decimation of our culture, our character, and our communities.

Through my understanding of what it means to be Two-Spirit, to be ennvrkvpv, I feel more alive and confident in my body. Knowing there is a place for me in my culture, in my community, gives me a sense of connection, something I have deeply longed for. It is through this connection that I feel a calling to explore more. I have chosen the culture of sexuality, and in particular Indigenous sexuality, to explore somacultural liberation because my identity exists in the intersections of sexuality, Indigeneity, settler identity, and colonization. Plus, I am fascinated by all aspects of sexuality—identity, behavior, and the power of pleasure to heal.

LET'S TALK ABOUT SEX

Can sexuality be owned the same way we think of ownership in terms of land? If so, sexuality can also be stolen and colonized. Indigenous people across the globe continue to thrive despite efforts of colonizers to steal their land, destroy their culture, and eradicate their humanity, including their sexuality. The conditions upon which Indigenous people, in what is now known as North America, thrive despite colonization are worthy of exploration and dissemination and should be inclusive of 2SLGBTQIA+ resilience narratives. The concept of decolonizing sexuality is not taken lightly, nor is it to be used as an appropriation of other decolonizing movements among Native American and First Nations people. Finley (2011) posits, "heteropatriarchy and heteronormativity should be interpreted as logics of colonialism" (p. 33), and Jolivétte (2016) adds, "changing cultural beliefs and values relating to gender, sexuality, religion, and membership all contribute to internalized United States hegemonic form of sovereignty" (p. 73). Additionally, the concept of decolonizing sexuality is not exclusive to this book, nor am I claiming ownership of the phrase. Decolonization and decolonizing sexuality impact colonized people across the globe and include issues such as land, water, agriculture, food, sex, gender, and sovereignty.

There is debate around the usage of the word *decolonize* in regard to anything other than the land. Although I believe it is important to acknowledge the land that was stolen from Indigenous people (including my family), it is also important to acknowledge the injurious impact colonization continues to play in the lives of Indigenous people today. Tuck and Yang (2012) posit, "decolonization is not a metaphor" (p. 1) and further clarify by stating, "when metaphor invades decolonization, it kills the very possibility of decolonization; it re-centers Whiteness, it resettles theory, it extends innocence to the settler, it entertains a settler future" (p. 3). This proclamation does not allow for the decolonization movement to expand to its fullest possibility. Limiting usage of decolonization rhetoric maintains setter colonialism by focusing only on the land and evading the trauma experienced by descendants of Indigenous genocide. Tuck and Yang ascertain "decolonize (a verb) and decolonization (a noun) cannot easily be grafted onto pre-existing discourses/frameworks, even if they are critical, even if they are anti-racist, even if they are justice frameworks" (p. 3). Through critical analysis, engagement with community leaders, and recognizing gaps in the literature, the concept of decolonizing sexuality is directly linked to the land as it was experienced pre-contact. Jolivétte

(2016) states, "to decolonize gender and sexuality . . . requires a releasing of each of the epistemological narratives that limit the definitions of what it means to be Native, mixed-race, Two-Spirit, and/or queer" (p. 47). An enmeshment with the mentality of the colonizers begins early in primary socialization settings with parents or primary caregivers. These belief systems are perpetuated in secondary socialization settings such as schools, religious institutions, or public spaces (i.e., parks, retail establishments, etc.). Children learn about the myths of Thanksgiving and Pocahontas while in elementary school, yet Native American history is largely erased from the education system in the United States.

In 1995, the Walt Disney Company released the animated film *Pocahontas*, which further perpetuated the romanticized story of an Indigenous woman saved by the love of a White man. When Disney chose the story of Pocahontas, it was the first time they had chosen a real-life figure (Matoaka, of the Algonkian tribal nation, aka Pocahontas) to transform into an animated film. In the Disney version, Pocahontas is transformed from an adolescent into a young woman, and John Smith is transformed into a much younger man. Disney's *Pocahontas* "transforms colonialism into a benevolent ideology of good will, proto-environmentalism, proto-feminism, and cross-cultural tolerance . . . [and] . . . suggests that colonialism was simply one manifestation of today's preferable multicultural world" (Buescher & Ono, 1996, p. 257). Disney's version of Pocahontas perpetuates the claim that the land was empty and thus for the taking, which is extended to possession of the Native body and of one's sexual sovereignty. This possession is apparent in the possession of Native male sexuality as we see Kocoum (portrayed as Pocahontas's soon-to-be husband) shot and killed, leading to the capture of John Smith and the intervention of Pocahontas to save Smith's life. Simpson (2017) states, "since we came from societies where sexual freedom and self-determination of our bodies was our birthright, the control of our bodies and sexuality became of critical importance to the colonizers" (p. 110). Disney's *Pocahontas* can be experienced as the exotification of Indigenous bodies, the sexualization of Native women, and the desexualization of Native men. This narrative offers an example of why decolonizing sexuality and making a claim for sexual sovereignty are important. It is necessary to see Native sexualities as being as complex as other racial and ethnic groups.

Morgensen (2015) ascertains "colonial masculinities arose to violently control and replace distinctive gender systems among Indigenous peoples" (p. 38) and "colonial masculinity sustains both colonial and heteropatriarchal power by presenting its victims as the cause and proper recipients of its own violations" (p. 55). This subjugation is extended into the concept of "heteropatriarchy and heteronormativity . . . as logics of colonialism" (Finley, 2011, p. 33).

In 2005, Wilson and Yellow Bird edited *For Indigenous Eyes Only: A Decolonization Handbook*. They state in their introduction, "the first step toward decolonization is to question the legitimacy of colonization" (p.3). This question around legitimacy is applicable to sexuality because it welcomes a critique of the discourse surrounding sexological understandings of how colonizing perspectives of gender and sexual orientation are rampant in the fields of anthropology and psychology. Wilson and Yellow Bird (2005) further their position by stating, "current institutions and systems are designed to maintain the privilege of the colonizer and the subjugation of the colonized, and to produce generations of people who will never question their position within this relationship" (p. 1). The privilege of the colonizer can be seen in academic discourse when the history of sexuality is started from, and explained through, a Eurocentric perspective, without acknowledging multiple ways of acquiring and disseminating knowledge.

In 2012 Wilson and Yellow Bird released *For Indigenous Minds Only: A Decolonization Handbook*, and added to their previous work by positing this:

> *Colonization refers to both the formal and informal methods (behavioral, ideological, institutional, political, and economical) that maintain the subjugation and or exploitation of Indigenous peoples, lands, and resources. Decolonization is the meaningful and active resistance of the forces of colonialism that perpetuate the subjugation and or exploitation of our minds, bodies, and lands. Decolonization is engaged for the ultimate purpose of overturning the colonial structure and realizing Indigenous liberation. (p. 3)*

From this framework, to decolonize sexuality means to dismantle exploitative practices, policies, and discourse that subjugate and colonize the sexuality of Indigenous people, including those who identify as LBGTQ+ and/or Two-Spirit. Finley (2011) states, "all sexualization of

Native peoples constructs them as incapable of self-governance without a heteropatriarchal influence that Native peoples do not naturally possess" (p. 35). Self-governance is an extension of agency. Agency is inclusive of sexual agency, which is an extension of sovereignty of the body, mind, and spirit. Rifkin (2011a) adds to the discourse stating, "decolonization partially entails a changed understanding of the relation between sexuality and sovereignty, in which the former does not serve as a basis for exiling people from inclusion in the latter" (p. 174). For this changed understanding to disseminate across tribal nations, the process of decolonizing sexuality is not limited to the individual, but rather includes tribal communities, tribal nations, and tribal leadership. The process of decolonization is not limited only to the land, but rather it must be evaluated from the multiple aspects in which Indigenous people have been impacted by colonization, which includes the critical examination of sexual sovereignty, what Smith (2011) calls, "unsettling settler colonialism" (p. 43).

Decolonization, including decolonizing sexuality, is a process of reclamation wherein those who have survived genocide engage in ceremony and advocate social and sexual justice issues, which uplift Indigenous people and serve as a part of the healing process. According to Tuhiwai Smith (1999), "decolonization . . . does not mean and has not meant a total rejection of all theory or research or Western knowledge. Rather, it is about centering our concerns and world views and then coming to know and understand theory and research from our own perspectives and for our own purposes" (p. 39). A part of the knowing and the understanding Smith (1999) advocates for must be inclusive of diverse cultural perspectives on gender and sexuality in North America pre- and post-contact. Not including sexuality in the discussion around decolonization would result in a similar sterile paradox and perpetuate the exotification of Native desire.

It is important to situate sexuality (which includes gender, sexual orientation, sexual behaviors, sexual health, and vitality, as well as culture) as part of the conversation when discussing colonization. Due to the compound trauma experienced by Native Americans/First Nations people, the negative ramifications of colonization continue to impact Indigenous people, in particular Native women and Two-Spirit-identified Native people. To shift the rhetoric around concepts of colonization toward human sexuality, it is important to examine the discourse that perpetuates the exotification of Indigenous people.

An issue that is greatly impacting Indigenous people is missing and murdered Indigenous women. The movement known as Missing and Murdered Indigenous Women (MMIW) is a multitribal nation effort to find missing Indigenous women and a call for justice for all Indigenous women who have been murdered. The MMIW movement first gained traction in Canada in 2015, though the issue of missing and murdered Indigenous women has been ongoing since the invasion of 1492. The MMIW movement has also grown to now include Indigenous girls, Two-Spirits, and men. The acronym can also be seen as MMIWG2SP, or MMIP, though most often MMIW is still being used and is inclusive of all Indigenous people who continue to suffer horrible injustices. The MMIW movement is also connected with environmental justice issues. Environmental issues such as oil fracking and pipelines often exist on or near Native reserves and reservations. Statistics show a high incidence of Indigenous people going missing or being found murdered near what are being called "man camps" (Sovereign Bodies Institute, n.d.). Man camps are small communities built near the sites of oil fracking or pipelines that consist of large numbers of men, many of whom are on site without their families (if they are married/partnered) or are single.

In the United States, crimes that are committed by non-Native people on reservations must be tried by state or federal court. This means violent crimes committed on a reservation against Indigenous people (rape, murder, etc.) cannot be tried by a tribal court. In *Oliphant v. Suquamish Indian Tribe* (1978) the United States Supreme Court ruled "Indian" tribal courts hold no jurisdiction over "non-Indian" people. An exception to this law was passed in 2013 as part of the reauthorization of the Violence Against Women Act and took effect in 2015, granting tribal courts jurisdiction to prosecute domestic violence and dating violence issues. Because other violent crimes cannot be prosecuted by tribal courts, MMIW/MMIP cases that happen on tribal lands are held up by bureaucracy with many cases never coming to trial.

Violence against Indigenous women is rarely covered by mainstream media, whereas violence against White women is. An example includes the recent missing and murdered case of Gabby Petito, a twenty-two-year-old White woman who was murdered by her fiancé. Gabby's case gained international attention and efforts were coordinated on a national level to find her murderer. Gabby's case is tragic and horrific, and I mean no disrespect to her family, friends, or people who worked to find justice on her behalf. I am pointing out that it is unfortunate MMIW cases do not receive the same efforts to find justice. Nor are the same efforts given to Black women, Asian women, Latin and Hispanic women. This is because our culture values certain bodies over others.

In October 2020, Savanna's Act, aka Public Law No. 116-165, was passed by the United States Congress. Savanna's Act directs the Department of Justice (DOJ) to "review, revise, and develop law enforcement and justice protocols to address missing or murdered Native Americans" (S.227 - Savanna's Act, 2020). Savanna's Act is the first congressional action taken to specifically address MMIW/MMIP and more efforts are needed to ensure safety for Indigenous people, on and off tribal lands.

Indigenous people continue to experience harm from ongoing colonial efforts impacting Indigenous sexuality. The culture we live in, a culture of colonization and normalizing violence, means Indigenous people will continue to be harmed by efforts to force Indigenous people to assimilate to dominant cultural values, which themselves were based upon greed, violence, and using religion as the excuse to cause harm. Somacultural liberation requires all of us to recognize that the culture we currently live in was created. This means we can create a new culture—a culture in which people are allowed to thrive, and equality and equity are at the center of everything we do moving forward.

I do not anticipate the practice of somacultural liberation will mean Indigenous people will have our lands returned to us, or that we will no longer suffer from sexual violence. My hope is that by naming the truths in parts of my identity, you will learn truth about your identity, and together we can create new identities and move toward liberation together.

6

SOMACULTURAL LIBERATION

In 2018 I was given an opportunity to teach at a university in the Bay Area of California. One of the courses that I had been offered to teach was Multicultural Counseling and the Family. Readers in the mental health field are apt to be familiar with this or a similarly titled course, as it is a requirement for any mental health graduate-level student. This is the cultural buffet class, as I like to call it. In my case, I was given eight weeks to cover an array of mental health topics as they related to culture. The cultural piece excited me. How others viewed culture in the context of a multicultural counseling class would understandably be a challenge.

I say *understandably* because I myself took a multicultural counseling course while I was in graduate school, and I remember feeling disappointed that the cultural groups I was interested in working with (Indigenous, sexual minorities) were barely represented in the course material. Truthfully though, how could they be? The majority of professional development courses in psychotherapy, self-help, and coaching all consciously choose to continue valuing Western ideologies of treatment and healing as being superior to others. This ethnocentric perspective shows up in the exchange between doctor/therapist/social worker/coach and client. It may be less evident when the parties have similar and/or shared cultural experiences such as age, gender, and where they grew up. However, greater cultural misunderstandings can be seen in those who differ in their backgrounds and take little to no interest in understanding the varying intersections of a client's identity, let alone their own.

When I was looking for material for the multicultural counseling class I was going to teach, I came across the work of Pamela Hays whose book *Addressing Cultural Complexities in Counseling and Clinical Practice: An Intersectional Approach* (2022) became foundational in the course. Hays introduced me to the ADDRESSING model, an acronym she created to bring greater awareness to the intersecting aspects of a client's identity. Hays, a White cis-gender heterosexual female, was also teaching multicultural counseling classes when she recognized students' needs for clinical information relevant to providers and clients of diverse, complex, and intersecting identities. Hays created the ADDRESSING acronym and framework to bring greater awareness to the intersecting aspects of clients' identities and systems of privilege/oppression.

The ADDRESSING model stands for age, disability (life-long), disability (acquired), religion, ethnicity and race, sexual orientation, socioeconomics, Indigeneity, nation of origin and nationality, and gender. I resonated with the ADDRESSING model and used it as a way to diversify the readings for the course I was teaching. I did not want to fall into a similar pattern of giving my students an article about how to do therapy with (fill in the blank) population. Instead, I planned to give my students articles on aging in Black communities, sex therapy with clients living with a disability, Two-Spirit narratives on health and wellness, Audre Lorde's *Uses of the Erotic*, community mental health initiatives, Missing and Murdered Indigenous Women, refugee populations in the Midwest of the United States, and Two-Spirit-affirmative, trans-affirmative, gender non-conforming-affirmative, and gender non-binary-affirmative mental healthcare.

While I was preparing for the course, including while I was finding articles, podcasts, and videos to fit the theme of each week, I began to notice that something was missing from the Hays ADDRESSING model.

One morning while in a Pilates reformer class, I remember being in a lunge position with my right leg forward. My hands were above my head and my right leg was trembling from the stretch. As I moved out of the pose, I said out loud, "body." I knew that body was something that I felt was missing from the Hays model. What is the client's relationship to their body and how others respond to their body? I thought B ADDRESSING sounded all right, but wondered what else might be missing. I then thought back to how Hays first created the ADDRESSING model while doing fieldwork with Alaska Natives. As an Indigenous person, I wanted anything that I offered to the field to have an Indigenous framework already centered in the model, which is one of the many things I appreciate about the ADDRESSING model. What this model is not clear on from the Indigeneity perspective is relationship to land. For non-Indigenous people, the I in the ADDRESSING model was one where they would say not applicable (N/A). I found this to be a form of bypassing or spiritual bypassing by not acknowledging their relationship or the benefits they have received from the genocide of the Indigenous peoples of the lands we now call the United States. How could I address this absence from the ADDRESSING model?

O is for occupy. Because I am centering Indigenous epistemologies in my work, and because I believe that it is crucial for collective healing to recognize the ongoing challenges and threats to sovereignty that Indigenous people continue to experience. What is your relationship to the Native people whose land you now occupy? If you have moved throughout your life, what was your relationship to the Native people whose land you used to occupy? Are you/were you a homeowner? What is that like for you to own land on stolen land? What is it like for you to pay rent to a landowner who may or may not be someone who identifies as Native American, First Nations, or Indigenous? If you are an Indigenous person who lives in a territory outside of your home territory, do these questions also apply to you?

I believe part of that inquiry may be found in reflecting on one's lifestyle. L is for lived experience, and I suggest adding this to the acronym because lived experience is, in part, reflective of one's culture or the dominant culture in which they were raised. Lived experience may include where someone lives and what values they ascribe to living there. Lived experience may also include what kind of relationships someone enters into—marriage, friendship, work-related. Lived experience also includes any traumas or significant life events someone may have experienced. I believe reflecting on our lived experiences, and how these experiences impact our bodily thoughts, feelings, sensations, and inquiries, grants us a depth of possibility in regard to self-growth and understanding. Lived experience is also indicative of my final suggestion in an amended acronym, desire.

D is for desire. In addition to framing my work from Indigenous epistemologies, I also see my work through the lens of sexuality, which I define as a multitudinous sphere of human expression, behavior, and identity. Desire encapsulates a breadth of experiences. Desire may be about what someone is currently doing regarding actively pursuing desire and/or pleasure, and/or what someone hopes to do or has challenges doing in regard to going after their desires. This may or may not include anything related to sexuality, though I value the idea that sexuality is deeply influenced by our cultural experiences and in turn may impact what, who, or how we have desires.

BTP (before the pandemic), I had an office in the Castro district of San Francisco. Several of my clients had commented on the negative reinforcing of tropes of desirable gay men, which to clients who identified as Black, Indigenous, or as a Person of Color (BIPOC), meant White, thin, muscular, or, depending on the time of year, White, hairy, thicker body. When these tropes of what is or what is not sexually appealing are continuously reinforced through advertisements promoting parties and community events, BIPOC 2SLGBTQIA+ people feel unseen, not valued, and have a unique combination of both a hyper- and a hyposexualized experience in the community. How does this impact how certain people think about desires and what they believe may or may not be accessible to them?

I have been teaching from a BOLD ADDRESSING framework for many years. As I am talking about the framework, perhaps you notice something else that is missing. If so, I encourage you to expand upon my expansion. Before writing this book, I arranged a meeting with Pamela Hays over Zoom. For our call, she was at her home in Alaska, and I was at my mother's home on the Poarch Creek Indians Reservation in the state now known as Alabama. Pamela generously supported my expansion of her ADDRESSING model to include the BOLD acronym. Thank you, Pamela.

The BOLD ADDRESSING model is one methodology of thinking about positionality and epistemology. Because positionality and epistemology are in a constant state of shifting, I encourage clients and workshop participants to have, at a minimum, a yearly practice of reflecting on their BOLD ADDRESSING assessment. To give you an idea of how you may incorporate this assessment, I am sharing mine with you. You will see how I have created a thought tree with my assessment. I encourage you to come up with your own. While you are going through yours, please pay attention to any thoughts, feelings, sensations, or inquiries that may arise.

Roger J. Kuhn

BOLD ADDRESSING

- **BODY**

  Stats: 5′ 11″, 185 lbs., silver hair, dark-brown eyes, olive-tan skin, two surgeries (gallbladder [at age 23] and hernia [at age 22]), intermittent seasonal allergies

  Adornments: Three tattoos, left ear pierced

  Skills: Flexible, can walk for many miles before tiring, enjoy physical exercise, enjoy touch (giving and receiving), able to use my body in ways that feel good to me (singing, dancing, having sex)

  Relationship: Recovered from an eating disorder; intermittent body dysmorphia; appreciative of strength, recovery, and healing; sometimes worry that I am too tan; sometimes worry that I am unattractive because of my body size; sometimes worry that I will have similar health ailments to those other members of my family have experienced

Sex: Experience somatic, intellectual, and emotional functioning that is congruent with how I would like to express myself sexually

- **OCCUPY**

This book is written in the traditional homelands of the Poarch Creek, Ohlone, Pomo, and Kumeyaay people.

I was born and raised in the lands of the Očhéthi Šakówiŋ people. When we were growing up, my mother would often take us to the White Earth Reservation for doctor and dentist appointments. My parents were also friends with other Native people, some of whom were members of the tribal nation on whose stolen land we lived. Later in my youth, my family would live for a couple of years on our traditional homelands in the state now known as Alabama. It was during this time in my life that I became immensely interested in what it meant to be Native American, and specifically, what it meant to be Poarch Creek.

I currently split my time between Pomo territory in Guerneville, CA, and Ohlone territory in San Francisco. My relationship to the Native people of this land is varied. Because of policies like Public Law 959 also known as The Indian Relocation Program/Adult Vocational Training Programing of the 1950s, urban areas like San Francisco have large Native American populations that may or may not be representational of the original Native people who occupied the land. San Francisco has a relatively large urban Native population, and the Ohlone people are not federally recognized. I do advocacy work for the Native community of the Bay Area, which includes the Ohlone and Pomo people. Some of the activities that I have participated in to be of service to the Native community in the Bay Area include being a community organizer of the Bay Area American Indian Two-Spirits Powwow, serving as a board member of the American Indian Cultural Center of San Francisco, and being a community representative for the San Francisco Human Rights Commission.

- **LIVED EXPERIENCE**

Relationship: Married to my husband, Sean, for fourteen years. Together for seventeen years. Mostly monogamous though we have had our shared experiences with others. Dated for two years before moving in with one another. We were in different socioeconomic groups when we started dating. I struggled with the discrepancy in finances because I worried that I would not be good enough since I didn't make as much money.

Family: My parents divorced when I was twenty years old. My mom tells me that my dad told her he would only sign divorce papers when I was past eighteen because he wouldn't pay any child support. My father died from a drunk driving car accident when I was twenty-three. I have a supportive and loving relationship with my mother and my three older sisters. I occasionally have some tension and ruptures with one of my sisters, though nothing that has ever been beyond repair.

Friends: My friendships are very important to me. I have had many of the same friends for the entirety of my adult life. My best friend, James, and I have been friends since I was fifteen years old. Most of my closest friendships are with people I have known for twenty-plus years. These are the people who have seen me when I was struggling to survive and they stood by my side, lifted me up, and supported me the best way they could. I love my friends and always prioritize them in my life. Important to note: I also consider my husband one of my best friends. I feel incredibly blessed to say that.

Education: I have a lot of certificates, diplomas, and degrees. My degrees include an associate degree in occupational studies, a bachelor's degree in anthropology, a master's degree in counseling psychology with an emphasis on somatic psychology, and a doctoral degree (PhD) in human sexuality with a concentration in clinical practice. I do not consider myself overly ambitious and I didn't pursue a PhD because I loved being in school and learning. For a long time, education was a source of shame for me. I didn't go to college after high school and believed that I was destined to be poor my entire life because of it. I also wasn't able to afford to pay for school and support myself; I needed to have a full-time job in order to survive. Once I committed myself to pursuing a college degree, I did so to better myself in the world, and also as a way to honor my ancestors who were not given the option to go to school, let alone obtain an advanced degree. Native American people remain underrepresented in academic spaces including as students, faculty, and administrators. Greater representation and more diversified curricula are needed to ensure barriers are removed.

Creative: I live a creative lifestyle, which I define as one that prioritizes the making, sharing, witnessing, participating in, and exploring of a variety of expressive ways to live life. My main form of creative expression has always been music, including song-writing, singing, playing musical instruments, and performing.

Work: I have had a variety of jobs throughout my life: entry-level positions, various restaurant jobs, go-go dancer, musician, professor, therapist, retail worker, massage therapist, yoga instructor. Only in the past couple of years have I felt that I am doing work that resonates more with who I am and how I want to be in the world. I enjoy public speaking, teaching, and helping people who are in challenging places in their lives. I also really love being my own boss (mostly). A strong work ethic is something I remember hearing about when I was growing up. I remember when I interviewed for my first job in New York, I mentioned to the person doing the interview that I was born and raised in North Dakota, which meant I had a strong work ethic. I got the job. Work and education are inextricably linked for me. In many of my past jobs, I felt stuck, with nowhere to go, because all of the other positions in the companies I was working for required an advanced degree of some kind. No college education meant less money. I know this isn't always true, though for many of us, we are raised with this as a cultural norm.

- **DESIRE**

  Where to begin? Sometimes I feel that I have too many desires, too many wants. I have entered a phase in my life where I can reflect more on the things that I desire and question whether they are true desires, cultural desires, or intergenerational desires. My desires include everything from a long, healthy, and prosperous life, to living in a cabin in the middle of the woods with a swimmable lake outside my door that also leads to a secret beach with beautiful tropical weather. Some desires are more attainable than others, and some desires are meant to be pure fantasy. I allow myself to have both. I desire to be adored. I desire to be loved. I desire to have pleasurable experiences daily. I desire to decolonize and unsettle. I desire to be creative and share my creativity with others. I desire to be seen and I desire to see others. I desire to frolic among the mountain gorillas. I desire to swim with whales. I desire world peace and the end to violence. I desire liberation.

I want to pause here for a moment of reflection. As I have been writing, I have been paying attention to the sensations in my body. I notice that I feel excited when I am reflecting on my BOLD ADDRESSING assessment. There are so many stories within each reflection. Here's an important thing to remember and embody about a somacultural liberation practice; stories are important, how we feel about those stories is more important. Our memory can only hold so many details. We may forget certain information about a story, though rarely do we forget how we feel about this information. From a clinical perspective, I believe there is so much rich information to explore with clients around how they feel about the aspects of their BOLD ADDRESSING assessment. Sometimes, when someone does this assessment, it is the first time they have ever sat and reflected upon their identity, the meaning they make of it, how they feel about it, and how it shifts how they may or may not interact with someone or something else.

- **AGE**

  Born in 1976, year of the American Bicentennial. Age is important in the BOLD ADDRESSING assessment model because part of understanding your positionality and epistemology is reflecting upon what may have been going on culturally in certain times across your life span. Something that I think about in my life is growing up in the 1980s, knowing that I was gay, and fearing that I would grow up and die from AIDS because the message that I was receiving as a child was if you were gay, you would die from AIDS. The ignorance, stigma, and shame were experienced by millions and resulted in deleterious impacts that are still being felt today.

  I also believe that being in my mid 40s is beneficial to my career as a therapist, educator, and public speaker. Culturally, we have a tendency to give a certain esteem to older people as if age somehow automatically makes you wiser. Age does not equate to life experience or wisdom.

- **DISABILITY (LIFE-LONG)**

  I do not have any life-long disabilities. Living with a disability is rarely something I thought about before working as an educator and a therapist. I recognize I have work to do around ableism and I commit to an ongoing learning process to ensure I am reflecting on my own positionality, privilege, and power.

- **DISABILITY (ACQUIRED)**

  I have minor hearing loss that, at present, does not require any further medical intervention. Having minor hearing loss may not qualify as a disability to some, though I add it here because it has impacted many of my passions, including public speaking and music. I have never equated my hearing loss to an actual disability and often feel a lot of shame when I mention to people that I have trouble hearing at times.

- **RELIGION**

  I currently do not have any religious affiliation.

  I was baptized as a Roman Catholic at around one year of age. My parents raised me in the Catholic Church through sixth grade. I attended summer school with nuns and went through the rituals of communion and confirmation. I regret not being an altar boy.

  When my parents separated, my mom started to take us to a new church, an Assembly of God. They seemed a lot happier than Catholics and I liked the songs we would sing. We later moved to Alabama, and I started to attend church services with my grandmother, Auntie Mabel, and Auntie Deb. I loved going to church, mostly for the singing, and also for the family time.

  When we left Alabama and moved back to North Dakota, my parents were still separated, and my mom chose not to take us to any churches or ever talk about religion. I occasionally went to a Catholic service with my friend Bree or Aunt Jean, though by that point in my adolescence, I had grown weary of Christianity and its many sects.

I spent my teen years fascinated with Wicca, tarot cards, and astrology.

In my adult life, I have been a practicing Buddhist and have attended an Interfaith church and seminary school. I dropped out of seminary school after one year. Rev. Rog wasn't cutting it for me.

- **ETHNICITY/RACE**

  I identify as a mixed-race Poarch Creek Native American. My mother, I, and all of my siblings are enrolled members of the Poarch Creek Indians, a federally recognized sovereign nation in the state now known as Alabama. My father is European American with German-Russian ethnicity.

  I have struggled with my mixed-race identity for the majority of my life.

  To some I look like the colonizer, to some I look like the colonized.

- **SEXUAL ORIENTATION**

  I identify as Two-Spirit, gay, and sexually fluid. Before learning about Two-Spirit I identified as gay, though I did not feel the label represented me well. I also recently began identifying as sexually fluid. I use this term to express my sexual attraction and desire for people of multiple gender identities. I use a lowercase g in gay because I once learned from a wise friend, Yamonte, capital G gay was representational of dominant cis-White males and the often-toxic culture that encapsulates the identity. The moment I heard that, it was all lowercase g for me going forward.

- **SOCIOECONOMICS**

  My family struggled financially for most of my childhood. We lived on a farm that my father inherited from his father (thanks to a card game bet). When my parents separated, we struggled even more financially and survived on food stamps and other government subsidies. My first seven years in New York I was poor, like digging-in-the-sofa-for-change poor. Like surviving-on-a-dollar-slice-of-pizza-and-a-bottle-of-Yoohoo-a-day poor. Like almost-evicted-from-my-apartment poor. I landed a good-enough paying job in my late twenties whereafter I no longer felt I was struggling as much and could put a little bit of money away for savings. When I was thirty I met my husband, who at the time was already a successful lawyer with a beautiful condo he owned in the Chelsea neighborhood of New York City. After two years of dating, we moved in together and I was now living in a doorman building in what I thought was one of the coolest neighborhoods in town (also one of the most 2SLGBTQIA+ friendly). In the seventeen years that Sean and I have been together, our wealth has increased, and at the time of this writing, my name is on the deed to two homes in California, and I drive a BMW convertible that I paid for myself. Despite no longer being poor, I continue to struggle with scarcity mentality and believe part of my work ethic has been generated as a reaction to the trauma I have in my life about surviving in poverty.

- **INDIGENEITY**

  I am an enrolled member of the Poarch Creek Indians, a sovereign nation located in the state now known as Alabama. I have a strong relationship and connection to my Indigenous identity. Even though I am mixed-race (White father), I have always considered myself Native first.

  I am connected to my tribal communities and return to our homeland territories, including our reservation, several times a year.

I am working on what it means for me to have an active practice of decolonization (and unsettling).

- **NATION OF ORIGIN**

I was born on July 11, 1976, in Fargo, ND. Fargo is in the original territory of the Očhéthi Šakówiŋ people.

Being raised in the United States as both an Indigenous person of Poarch Creek ethnicity and an American person with mixed-race German Russian/Creek ethnicity was a challenging experience. I understand the America-first mentality, though I never resonated with it. I do not care much for White-washed Eurocentric histories of the United States. I do not identify with flying an American flag at my home, on my vehicle, in my classroom, or anywhere, for that matter, other than outside of government entities.

From my perspective as a Two-Spirit Poarch Creek person, my nation of origin is the Muscogee nation. Legally, that is not relevant to the United States and I must declare myself a citizen of the United States.

I have never had a desire to serve in the US military. When I was eighteen and needed to register for the draft, I absolutely dreaded it. I feared that I would be forced to fight for a country that had massacred my ancestors and continue to hurt my people. At that time in US history, the military had a policy of "Don't Ask, Don't Tell" regarding sexual orientation. Not only would I be forced into serving a country that considers me and my people less than, but they also expected me to lie about who I was.

- **GENDER**

I identify as ennvrkvpv Two-Spirit Indigiqueer. I use he/him pronouns, though if used with good intention, I also welcome she/they/girl/boy/Mr./Miss/Mrs.

My relationship to gender has changed a lot over the years. Gender identity was something that traumatized me as a child. I was constantly being called a girl as a pejorative. I was also called queer, femme, pussy, sissy. These words, sometimes spoken by my father toward me, always hurt because I knew they were meant with malice, though I was never really hurt by the words themselves. From early in my understanding of my life, I have never felt like a boy or a girl; I have always felt somewhere in between. In the Muscogee language our word ennvrkvpv translates to "in the middle," which I understand to be culturally relevant to how I choose to identify. I also credit my mom and sisters, who never discouraged me from expressing what some would call my feminine side. To them I was just being Rog. I have always seen my mom and my sisters as strong independent people. Which is why when someone uses aspects of identity that are often ascribed to women as pejoratives, I would soothe myself by saying, "women are powerful, women are amazing, I am from a woman."

Cis-straight men who use feminine pejoratives against others are getting it all wrong. Don't they love vulvas and vaginas and pussy? Aren't those the things so many have gone to wars over? Don't they covet vulvas above anything else? I think the word they are looking for is *asshole*. I believe that is a better word because assholes are what they fear most. They fear assholes (anuses) most because they hate that they feel occasional pleasure from that part of their body. Many cis-straight men have been indoctrinated into a culture that has taught them to believe anal pleasure equates to being gay, gay equates to being weak, weak equates to being less than, being less than equates to oppression. They should start using *asshole* more often as it is truly more aligned with the toxic masculinity that they perpetuate every time they use one of these pejoratives.

As you have read, my BOLD ADDRESSING assessment is fairly robust. I gave you just an example of what yours or a client's might look like. When I do this exercise in workshops, I often give people 10 minutes to do a quick BOLD ADDRESSING assessment and have them reflect upon anything they may be aware of that might influence how they participate and what they retain and/or share from the workshop. This begins a conversation around culture as a primary foundation to understanding our positionality and epistemology. As I go back and read what I have shared with you, I notice the sensations I feel in my body. I notice a tightening and constriction in my throat when I reread something that I worry may be too revealing about myself. I notice a fluttering sensation in my belly and chest when I reread something that I enjoy sharing about myself.

A BOLD ADDRESSING assessment can be done within a short time span of 10 minutes and/or the assessment can be done in greater depth and detail. I worked on mine for close to 3 hours and there is still much more I could write. I enjoy learning using multiple approaches including visual, auditory, didactic, hands-on, and self-reflection. When I do a BOLD ADDRESSING, I am learning about myself. I then have a key that I can use to better understand the somatic reactions and sensations I experience when I encounter certain phenomena in my life. In the Intro to Psychology course I took as an undergrad student, I learned correlation does not mean causation. I do agree with this to some extent, yet I also strongly believe our varying cultural experiences have differing impacts on our bodies, which in turn may cause us to behave and/or react in certain ways.

Experiential: Growth Work

Take a minimum of 30 minutes to complete this exercise. You are going to do your own BOLD ADDRESSING assessment. You can write a lot of information, or minimal information, in any of the categories. You can also include somatic sensations, thoughts, feelings, and inquiries that arise around any of the themes.

Extra credit: Choose a family member, friend, or community member to share your BOLD ADDRESSING assessment with. Share any insight you may have gained about yourself by going through the assessment. Write about or share how understanding who you are is helpful in what you know about the world around you.

POSITIONALITY, PRIVILEGE, AND POWER

The BOLD ADDRESSING assessment helps us recognize intersections of our identity. It is in these intersections that the processing begins. The BOLD ADDRESSING assessment is fluid as aspects of our identity continue to shift over time (such as age and lifestyle). This also means that sometimes intersections of our identity hold power (age and gender) and grant us certain privileges based upon what is determined to be in the best interest of those in powerful positions. I call this combination the *Triple Ps*, positionality, privilege, and power.

As addressed in the BOLD ADDRESSING assessment, *positionality* is our identity in the here and now, influenced by the past and our future aspirations. Depending on various intersections of our positionality, we may or may not have certain privilege that grants access to power. In my case, an example of this may be my perceived gender (male), which brings me to a higher degree of privilege in the United States. Then, intersect my gender with my mixed-race identity (Native and White), and suddenly I am no longer in a position of power based solely upon my gender. Now the hegemonic pecking order seeps into play, and due to my mixed-race status, I am relegated to less than in comparison to White males who, through conscious and subconscious ways, we have been programmed to believe are the arbiters of privilege and power.

Privilege and *power* are also subjective terms. There are certain legal parameters that apply to privilege and power, as in an attorney/client relationship and judges holding power over judicial matters. Privilege and power are also contextual and subjective outside of legal parameters and have personal and collective meanings. White supremacy is an example of privilege and power being used in ethnocentric and deleterious ways that impact others in manners resulting in genocide, enslavement, and land theft. A reverse of this would be looking at community organizing around BIPOC's liberation in the United States. If our collective privilege and power come at a direct cost to others, we are perpetuating the same harm our ancestors did before us. If our personal privilege and power come at a direct cost to others, we are guilty of abusing our positionality and intentionally inflicting harm upon others.

I want to make an important distinction here regarding the Triple Ps. Black and Indigenous people may face increasing complexity when reflecting on their Triple Ps. This is, in part, due to the assimilation into White culture being treated as a privilege, thus granting certain power, in the United States. The reservation system upon which federally enrolled Native American people can choose to live, is an example of an assimilation attempt by the United States government. The reservation can only exist within the legal parameters established by the United States government. Although federally recognized tribal nations are considered sovereign, it is not a full sovereignty as the United States government is always the final arbiter. Assimilation was also a tool used by the United States government during the Indian Relocation Program, a federal program that encouraged Native people to take up vocational training in urban areas across the United States. Opponents of the act believe it was a continuation of government policies from the 1940s–1960s, which sought to eradicate tribal nations and assimilate Native people into the dominant White Euro-American culture. These attempts by the United States government are an extension of Andrew Jackson's Indian Removal Act of 1830, better known as the Trail of Tears, where the Seminole, Cherokee, Choctaw, Chickasaw, and Creek (Muscogee) people were forcibly removed from their homelands and relocated to what is now known as Oklahoma. Further assimilation policies by the United States government toward Native people are infamously embodied in the words of Captain Richard Henry Pratt who, in an 1892 speech at the National Conference of Charities and Corrections, stated a federal policy needed to be enacted to "kill the Indian . . . and save the man." These words were foundational in policies that created Indian boarding schools across the United States with the intention to Christianize, Americanize, and remove culture from Native people. These boarding schools were notorious for abuses inflicted upon Native children including rape and murder. Justice for these children and their families is an ongoing issue between the United States government and the Indigenous people of this nation.

If, according to our government, corporations have individual rights, then as a corporation, the United States government must be considered liable in the ongoing abuse of their power against all marginalized and oppressed people in this country.

I believe the Triple Ps impact all aspects of our lives. When we have privilege in one area of our lives, this does not guarantee power in other areas. For some people, this can lead to patterns of somatic dissociation, wherein the body becomes trained to contract when forced into a submissive or subversive position, whether that is by force or through a conscious and/or unconscious choice. Perhaps one of the reasons we see agitation when it comes to discussing issues around race and the intersection of identity is because these conversations challenge the dominant privilege and power narrative of White supremacy. The election of Barack Obama as the forty-fourth president of the United States was thought to be a radical turning point in the shift of power from the hands of White people (predominately men) and serve as a symbol that change was afoot. Though millions were inspired by his message of hope, the Obama presidency still perpetuated harm against Indigenous people by not acting quickly enough in opposing the Dakota Access Pipeline and the Standing Rock movement. The Obama presidency was still harmful to the 2SLGBTQIA+ community because it did not focus its efforts strongly enough advocating for equality in marriage rights, housing rights, employments rights, and enacting legislation to grant 2SLGBTQIA+ people equal treatment under the law. Supporters of the Obama administration will be quick to say that unfortunately not all groups or issues can be taken care of and that we should celebrate the accomplishments that can be shared by all. This kind of commentary often comes from people who do not have the same concerns for personal or community safety that I and other marginalized bodies do. I supported the Obama administration and still hold the belief that more could have been done to ensure safety for all.

Safety is also subjective. What does it mean to be safe and/or to feel safe? Is safe or safety a place, an action, a feeling? When I discuss being safe with people I work with, I need to be sure to understand how they define the word. Their positionality may impact how they feel about safety. When someone experiences varying kinds of trauma, personal or collective, it may impact how they feel safe in their body or around other bodies. Many of us have learned to regard other bodies, especially other bodies that do not look like ours, as potential threats. What about when we think our bodies do not look like they are supposed to or smell like they are supposed to? Sonya Renee Taylor (2018) calls this the body profit shame complex wherein we fall prey to the marketing gimmicks of multinational corporations who shame us into believing that our bodies are not pretty enough, sexy enough, thin enough, muscular enough, and so on in order to pressure us to spend billions of dollars annually to look, smell, and ultimately feel better about our appearances.

I could have written about somacultural liberation from the framework of marketing and the body profit shame complex and perhaps one day I will. One of the aspects I like about the somacultural framework is that it can be used by individuals, partners, friends, families, and communities from multiple dimensions and perspectives. My hope is that by sharing this theoretical ideology, I am enabling others to take inspiration from this work, apply it to their lives, and/or apply it to a larger sociocultural issue such as pretty privilege, thin privilege, and light-skin privilege, which are all extensions of positionality, privilege, and power. At varying times in our history (time being an important contextual reference in positionality), there have been differing popular opinions as to what is a more privileged bodily feature to have, and this is seen primarily when we focus on gender from a binary perspective. Reasons marketing companies like using a binary scale for gender are that 1) it is easier to do so than to focus on the multiplicity of gender identities someone may experience over their lifetime and 2) there is greater potential to use shame as a factor in how someone recognizes self outside of the idealized image of what they could be based upon a privileged position that grants access and power.

The Triple Ps are reflective of micro-, meso-, and macro-engagements with self, family and friends, and the larger communal structures we live in and with. One way to reflect upon this is to look at the people in your life. What is your relationship to your family of origin (this might include your parents, siblings, primary caregivers, or extended family members such as aunts, uncles, and cousins)? What is your relationship to your family of creation (this might include your friends, partner[s])? Do we stay in these relational configurations because they best exemplify our Triple Ps? If so, what aspects of our Triple Ps? What value do we place on relationality regarding positionality, privilege, and power? What value does hierarchical relationality offer us? Aristotle wrote of hierarchical relationality in his essay *Nicomachean Ethics* (330 BCE), wherein he described varying levels of friendship and the benefits of engagement at the various levels. He wrote

> *for the sake of pleasure or utility, then, even bad men may be friends of each other, or good men of bad, or one who is neither good nor bad may be a friend to any sort of person, but for their own sake clearly only good men can be friends; for bad men do not delight in each other unless some advantage come of the relation. (verse 4)*

I find his words relevant to the Triple Ps and to understanding some of the reasons we end up in or choose the relationships we are a part of in our lives. If someone will benefit in an advantageous way, positionality, privilege, and power will continue to be utilized to sort relational configurations into hierarchies. Knowing where someone falls and the reasoning behind their placement in a hierarchical configuration can be beneficial to understanding somatic, intellectual, emotional, and existential inquires that may arise.

If a primary human need is safety, what do we need to experience safety from a somatic, intellectual, emotional, or existential place? What values do we compromise to feel safer? Are we approaching safety from a perspective of compromise or collaboration? When we compromise, do we feel grief? I believe compromising with grief means giving up something you don't want to give up so you can reap benefits in another way. I believe collaboration differs from compromise because although it might include letting go of something, it offers more in the way of reaching a solution between self and something else.

Do subtle differences in words mean anything with regard to our perceptions? This too is a cultural consideration. Brené Brown's book *Atlas of the Heart* (2021) explores the impact of different words to describe emotional experiences. According to her research, we often use certain words interchangeably, though they have slightly different meanings.

CASHING IN YOUR TRIPLE P CHECK

I have never lived my life as a victim, though I have been victimized. From childhood abuse, relentless teasing in my adolescence because of my sexuality, and even dealing with White Supremacy ideology as a professor at a university in San Francisco, I have had my share of heart-breaking experiences that could have sidelined my growth. I did not move with these circumstances with ease; rather, I continue to feel the impact they have had on my life.

One of the ways I have learned to navigate the unfortunate circumstances I have encountered is by recognizing my Triple Ps and utilizing them in the best way to serve my higher good, while never intentionally causing harm to anyone else. Emphasis on *intentionality*. I have made some choice in my life that others did not like. I have been told the choices that I made to take care of myself were causing harm to other people. I do not subscribe to anyone's emotional blackmail and continue to stand by the choices that I have made.

In 2018, I began a job as a core faculty member of a graduate-level psychology program in the Bay Area. I was incredibly excited to start my new position where I would be teaching courses on human sexuality, couples counseling, therapeutic communications, and the body in psychotherapy. But early on in my tenure at the university, I began to receive pushback from students who told me I was not doing enough for them. For example, while I was teaching a one-credit human sexuality course, I was accused of being a misogynist, homophobic, and a racist, and of intentionally inflicting harm on a White cis-male student. A group of students rallied together and sent me a letter (via my White, cisgender, straight colleagues) to deliver the news that they believed I need more training. Their reasons for accusing me of these horrific acts were that I taught a lesson on Two-Spirit people and not any other racial group, that I did not have enough course material on bisexual people, that I refused to give an extension to a female student who was weeks behind on her coursework, and that I did not allow a White cis-male to extrapolate on his dating woes while the class was having a discussion on sexual violence against women. I contemplated quitting but knew it would fuel their fodder and belief that I was somehow in the wrong. My colleagues were not supportive. Against my better judgment and because of some stubbornness, I refused to let them win and remained at the university, never acknowledging their letter or taking additional trainings per their suggestion.

A year later, I had another encounter with a White cis-male student who called me violent after I suggested to him that holding space for a BIPOC client who is coming to therapy because they are angry about the racism they are facing in their life was not enough. He was so enraged by my suggestion that he could do more that he blew up in the classroom and caused an uncomfortable scene for all of the students. He rallied one other student to go to the administration to say I was making them feel unsafe. He also demanded an opportunity to speak to me, which I denied. What he thought about me was none of my business. I tried to speak to my department chair as well as the provost of the university, and neither would recognize these attacks as racist or homophobic. None of my White straight colleagues were experiencing the level of verbal assaults I experienced. Mind you, they also did not teach courses that were triggering regarding sex, race, gender, class, and power. I finally had enough with the entitlement many of the students in that university felt and chose to resign at the end of spring semester in 2020.

Although I did enjoy teaching the courses I was assigned, I did not enjoy the additional emotional labor I was experiencing. Stepping away was easier because of my Triple Ps. My positionality (at that time) meant I had a graduate degree and a license to practice psychotherapy. My private psychotherapy practice was successful, and I made three times as much as a therapist as I did as a professor. I did not need the salary the school was paying me. My socioeconomic status was a privilege that meant I did not have to fear that I would not have enough money to pay my bills. I recognized I had a lot of power in the situation and chose to cash in my Triple Ps check. While I initially was angry, tearful, and frustrated when I walked away from this job, a few months after, I felt an immense feeling of relief. I also told myself I would never again put up with a job (or a student) who treated me the way that university did. It took knowing my Triple Ps and how they impacted this situation to feel the confidence to walk away. I had already begun teaching at another Bay Area university before I resigned and have had an amazing experience teaching there over the past three years. Sometimes we need to know when to cash in our Triple P check. Don't worry, you have several Triple P checks in your checkbook.

Experiential: Cashing in Your Triple P Checks

Think of an area in your life you are wanting to let go of. This could be a job, a relationship, or a behavior/habit that you believe is causing you harm. What aspects of your positionality may be beneficial to you in working with this circumstance? How can you use the privilege this aspect of your positionality grants you? How can you utilize your own power to make the necessary change you need to make in your life? Set aside 15 to 30 minutes to assess your BOLD ADDRESSING model and write or talk to a trusted confidant (therapist, partner, friend, etc.) to process this reflection.

PHYSICAL AND EMOTIONAL REGULATION

To aid in the writing of this book, I participated in a thirty-day writing practice. The creator of the program offered advice on how to focus, organize, and have fun writing a book. One of the tools he offered was to listen to the same album or playlist every time you sit down to write. Your brain will then make the connection between writing and the music. He also suggested music with no lyrics as words can cause the mind to become distracted and you may start to sing along instead of keeping focused on the task. I utilized the Pomodoro Technique of writing, which brackets writing into 25-minute blocks of time. It worked; you're reading the book!

For my music selection, I went with a playlist that I have been developing for years that contains some of my favorite instrumental tracks of a particular genre. My instrumental taste in music falls into what some would call space, ethereal, new-age, or spa music. I like music that makes me feel like I am floating. I like the way my body can easily regulate to this kind of music. Listening to ethereal music makes me want to close my eyes, take a deep breath, and allow my body to fall back into a state of regulation. I also found it great for writing. I named the playlist "Chill the Fuck Out" and its purpose is to help me regulate my system when I am feeling stressed, or when I am working on something that I would like to bring acute focus to. If you don't already have one, I encourage you to create your own "Chill the Fuck Out" playlist and incorporate any kind of music that helps bring your system to a more balanced and regulated state. I do not encourage people to make this playlist and then consider their problems solved, however. Instead, I encourage people to listen to a "Chill the Fuck Out" playlist as one way to access a more regulated system so they can do the necessary work to make choices that best align with their needs, values, and goals.

On the resources page of my website (somaculturalliberation.com), you can find a link to my playlist on Apple Music and Spotify.

Humans and animals of all kinds use varying ways to help regulate their nervous system. The nervous system is broken down into two different systems, *sympathetic* and *parasympathetic*. Some of us learned sympathetic as being fight or flight, and parasympathetic as rest and digest. I like to use these systems to help you/us better understand some of the reasons our bodies may feel certain sensations at certain times and during certain interactions. We feel these systems on micro and macro levels, and at certain times (such as during a political election), we feel them simultaneously. Some people experience many personal traumas. Some people have more collective traumas. Some people have both. From a physiological perspective, neither of these situations or scenarios is better, more relevant, or more important than the other. Our nervous systems are all highly susceptible to dysregulation. This is an evolutionary adaptation that has been passed down to us from our ancestors. Culture and the meaning we make of it also impact our nervous system and can cause dysregulation. When these issues intersect, it can be an incredibly dysregulating experience.

When an experience happens to us that is negative, hurtful, or painful on emotional or physical levels, we have an expression in English that is said to help the person or group better regulate their system—"Shake it off." To shake it off means to get rid of or be over something. The expression is also a literal instruction. Literally shake your body to bring your system to a greater place of regulation. Literally shake off the bad feelings, and shake off any physical sensations of pain or discomfort. If only it were that easy.

Animals in the wild, as well as those held in captivity and those that have been domesticated, will shake their bodies to help regulate their systems. This phenomena has been noted in Peter Levine's *Waking the Tiger* (2008) and documented in professional and amateur videos. A quick search on Google of animals shaking after trauma will pull up over eighty thousand videos. One that I found really interesting has close to five million views. The video is entitled "Impala in and slowly out of collapsed immobility" and, as of this writing, it was available on the YouTube platform. The video, uploaded by Jim Hoper, is a clip from a National Geographic special and shows an impala slowly getting up after a leopard attack. The impala begins to shake its body while resting on the ground and then slowly moves upright and then shakes more before it jumps up and runs away.

Like the impala, humans have a capability to regulate our nervous system by engaging in bodily movements that might include shaking, jumping, tapping, swinging, or vocalizing. Think back to a time when you bumped your leg or saw something disturbing. Did your body shake it off? Was this a conscious or unconscious movement? Are you aware of any movements that you make that help regulate your nervous system?

Have you ever seen someone else sustain an injury or experience something disturbing? Do you remember what you may have heard someone say to them to help them regulate their nervous system? Do you remember what you may have said? Likely you've heard someone say or you have told someone to shake it off regarding their pain. Perhaps you've even told yourself this. I have become pretty good at shaking it off. Shaking it off does not necessarily negate how painful or traumatic and/or disturbing something may be. But it does help our nervous system regulate in order for us to have greater capacity to assess our situation and make a choice about our experience. Sometimes the choice is to take a breath or take a step forward. A choice does not constitute a grand gesture of change or implementation. It is one step in a series to bringing our lived experiences in greater alignment with our values, goals, and dreams.

Our nervous system is a true wonder. I want to know more about it, how it functions, what it alerts us to, and how we can regain a sense of balance, regulation, and homeostasis. When I think about a somacultural framework, I am including nervous system regulation as foundational.

Many of us are experiencing nervous system dysregulation on personal and systemic levels. I would like to emphasize that the intention of a somacultural framework is not to bring everything to a perfect place of harmonious balance. Although it does sound lovely, I am somewhat of a realist and know many people will never even hear about this book. They will not learn how to reflect on their cultural experiences to help regulate their nervous systems. Some who do hear of the book may refuse to read it out of concern that the topic is too left of center. Everybody is on somebody's left side.

The sympathetic nervous system is responsible for the states of fight, flight, freeze, fawn, and flop. One way that I encourage clients I work with to think, feel, and sense into their sympathetic nervous system is to envision a Window of Tolerance. The Window of Tolerance was created by Dan Siegel (1999) to describe the best state of "arousal" or stimulation in which we can function and thrive in everyday life.

WINDOW OF TOLERANCE

Siegel (1999) conceptualized the Window of Tolerance (WOT) as an analytic tool useful in recognizing how the sympathetic nervous system responds to stimuli that may be evocative or triggering. You can find a handout of the WOT tool on my website. According to Siegel's theory, we are all operating within a Window of Tolerance, and external or internal stimuli can put us out of our Window of Tolerance, which can lead us to states of hyperarousal such as fight, fight, freeze, fawn, or flop, or states of hypoarousal such as depression. I like to think of the WOT as a scale of 0 to 10, with 0 being our most balanced state (homeostasis) and 10 being our most activated or triggered state. Once we hit a 10 on our WOT, we go out of the window and our sympathetic nervous system does what it does—fight, fight, freeze, fawn, or flop—to help us survive. What many do not realize is that when we are out of our WOT, trauma bonds and imprints to our system, which can lead to posttraumatic stress disorder, panic attacks, or major depressive episodes.

I believe using a WOT is beneficial from a somacultural liberatory framework because it allows us to check in with ourselves around challenging issues and learn to regulate our systems so that we do not move into states of dysregulation. I encourage you to add a WOT check-in as part of your daily morning practice. The WOT check-in requires you to ask yourself where you are today on a scale of 0 to 10. The closer you are to a 10, the more dysregulated your system is, which means any minor issue you encounter during the day has the potential to push you out of your WOT and lead to panic, anxiety, shutting down, or a depressive episode. The WOT is also subjective; my level 2 may be your level 6. Further, anyone who experiences depression and/or anxiety due to chemical imbalances in their system may be subject to a higher WOT score based on their physiological makeup.

WOT requires that we recognize where we are on a bidirectional spectrum. I like to think of the WOT as a bidirectional spectrum of 0 to 10 going up (anxiety), which I denote by a plus (+) symbol, and 0 to 10 going down (depression), which I denote by a minus (–) symbol. When I do my daily WOT check-in, most days I register at a level 2+, 1–. I usually have a little something coursing through my system (body pain, thought, emotion, important meeting, etc.) that is occupying more of my attention, causing a bit of anxiety or depression. Being close to homeostasis on either side of the spectrum gives me a lot of space to go about my day and encounter situations, issues, or other people that may be evocative for me. I tend to be more anxious than depressive, with more of my daily WOT activity registering on the + spectrum. This may differ for you (or your clients) who may operate more on the – spectrum, or a combination of +/– depending on their lived experience and where they may be on their healing journey. I operate well until I get to about a stage 7+ on my WOT. I have designated my stage 7 as the point on the WOT when I began to drop a lot of "F" bombs: fuck this, fuck that, what the fuck, who the fuck, how the fuck, and so on. I realize if I do not take action to regulate my system, I will likely be out of my WOT and will experience a major state of dysregulation that can lead me to hyperventilate, pass out, shut down, act out, or most likely say something I later regret and don't remember saying in the first place.

It is helpful to know what issues in your life you find evocative (triggering) to best understand how your system (somatic, intellectual, emotional) is impacted in your WOT. It is also helpful to know what helps your system regulate once you have experienced a challenging thought, emotion, or experience. Some issues I find evocative include seeing or reading stories in the news I find upsetting, having a rupture of some kind in any of my relationships (husband, family, friends), doubting myself, having others doubt me, and experiencing ethnocentrism. Things I find that help regulate my system and bring me closer to homeostasis (balance) include listening to my favorite songs, praying, having a good chat with someone I care about, dancing, spending time with my dogs, going for a walk, exercising, and playing video games.

Experiential: Window of Tolerance (WOT)

This experiential will likely take 10 to 15 minutes. Get your journal and take a deep breath. Use the WOT rating scale +/– 0 to 10 and determine where you are in the moment. I recommend only doing this experiential if you are not in a hyper- or hypoaroused state.

Take a deep breath. Reflect upon your life and any experiences you find evocative. These can be directly related to particular people or events, or a generalization. Make a list of issues, experiences, people, thoughts, feelings, body issues, and so on that you find evocative. Take a deep breath. Take another deep breath. Make a separate list of actions you can take to bring your system closer to a state of homeostasis.

FOUR SPACES (MEDICINE WHEEL)

I give full credence and respect to the Indigenous peoples who have created and centered the medicine wheel as an integral component of knowledge, healing, and wellness. The medicine wheel does not come from my Indigenous community, though we now use the knowledge and teachings of it as part of our community, as do many Indigenous nations.

The medicine wheel has been culturally appropriated by many Western practitioners who have benefited financially from the oppression of Indigenous knowledge systems. I want to make it very clear to my readers that I learned about the medicine wheel, what I also call *four spaces*, from my lived experience as an Indigenous person. I learned this valuable method from other Indigenous people. Though medicine wheel and four spaces ideology may be familiar to some readers of this book, I need to strongly emphasize that my knowledge of this system comes from and is inspired by Indigenous knowledge. Many different growth and self-help modalities use quadrants to help differentiate thoughts, feelings, opinions, and the like; not all of them have appropriated from the Indigenous medicine wheel.

Medicine wheels differ depending on the Indigenous culture that is using them. The medicine wheel is often represented in four colors (red, yellow, black, white), four directions (north, south, east, west), four seasons (winter, spring, summer, fall), and four experiences (body, mind, emotion, existential). The latter usage is where I draw my inspiration from and where the medicine wheel is often appropriated.

The first time I attended an American Association of Sexuality Educators, Counselors and Therapists (AASECT) conference I went to a workshop facilitated by a well-known sex educator and therapist. She used the medicine wheel in her presentation but gave no background information as to where the medicine wheel came from. She didn't even call it the medicine wheel, though she used all the concepts found in medicine wheel ideology. Years later, I had an opportunity for a one-on-one conversation with the facilitator of that workshop. She revealed to me that she has an Indigenous grandparent from Peru. I gently explained to her that she still has a responsibility to share where her teachings come from. She said to me, "Did you read my book?" Yes, I had read her book; it was required reading for a course I took in my doctoral studies. In fairness, she does mention the medicine wheel in her book, though she does not name it as an Indigenous knowledge system. I explained to her she was perpetuating harm to Indigenous people by not sharing with her predominately White audience where her information was coming from. She acknowledged the harm and we agreed to disagree.

In my clinical and education work, I use medicine wheel ideology to help people understand somacultural liberation. I use the term four spaces unless I am working with clients who identify as Native or Indigenous. I always share where the ideology of four spaces comes from so my clients understand how Indigenous knowledge is used and applicable to their lives, even if they are not Native. We spend time discussing cultural appropriation and cultural appreciation, and once we determine they understand the difference and are interested in using the four spaces model, we proceed with the experiential.

The four spaces represent body (soma), mind (thoughts), emotion (feelings), and existential (spirit). You can take any issue in your life (positive or negative) and use the four spaces to help yourself understand the impact it is having on your system. In my work as a psychotherapist, sex therapist, and sexuality educator, the four spaces have been invaluable in helping people reflect upon the challenges they are experiencing. The four spaces can be worked with as follows:

Body (Soma): In this space, list any complications you experience on a somatic level. Examples include body sensations, body movements, body experiences, and so on.

Mind (Thoughts): In this space, list any thoughts you may have about the issue(s) you are working with. Examples include "I think I'm not good enough," and "I believe everyone is looking at me."

Emotion (Feelings): In this space, list any feelings associated with the issue(s) you are working with. Examples include "I feel sad," "I am lonely," "It is upsetting," and similar statements.

Existential (Spirit): In this space, list questions that remain. Examples include "Will I ever find love?" "Will I ever get to a place of acceptance?"

Once a four spaces experiential is complete, I invite my clients to reflect upon what they are seeing in each of the spaces. Do any themes emerge? Were any of the spaces easier to work with? If so, what do they think that is about?

The following is an example of how I use the four spaces in my work. I usually use a white board and draw a large plus sign in the middle (a blank piece of paper will do just fine). You also don't need to draw it out; spatial learning is a preferred style of mine, and I like to see the visual of the shape and how each quadrant is filled with words and phrases. You can find a free copy of a four spaces worksheet, as well as additional information on the medicine wheel, on my website, somaculturalliberation.com.

I will now use the four spaces to exemplify an ongoing challenge I have experienced throughout my life—biracial identity.

Body: Skin color, eye color, body size, body shape, penis size, weight, hair color, attractiveness, gallbladder, heart condition, diabetes, obesity, contraction, tightness, tingling, fitness level

Mind: I believe I am not Native enough. I assume people will ask about my name. I believe people will say I am too light-skinned to be considered Native. I expect White people will ask how much or what percent Native I am. I believe I will have the same genetic issues my Native family has. I think being a biracial person is complicated. I think I will always have to fight for inclusion. I assume I will never get to play a Native person in film or on television. I expect people will anticipate that I can speak my Native language. I believe White people exotify me. I think Native people are unsure about me. I believe I have a responsibility to always be Native first. I think if I don't mention that I am Native, people will assume that I am some other race/ethnicity.

Emotion: I feel conflicted. I feel angered. I feel sad. I feel anxious all the time. I feel disappointed a lot. I feel confused. I feel contemplative. I feel isolated. I feel lonely. I feel alone. I feel empowered. I feel proud.

Existential: Will I ever feel balanced? Will society ever get to a point where race does not matter? Will people ever stop judging me? Will anyone ever understand what it is like to be biracial? Will anyone understand what it is like to be mixed Native and White? Will people accept me and be interested in my work because it is interesting and not because I am Native?

The four spaces I shared are a mere snapshot of how the issues of biracial identity impact my system. There is certainly more I could say about each of the four spaces because I am always discovering new somatic, intellectual, emotional, and existential experiences to add. In combination with my BOLD ADDRESSING assessment, the four spaces help me understand how the complexity of my identity impacts my overall lived experience. The four spaces do not exist in isolation.

The medicine wheel teaches that all things are connected. Our bodies, our minds, our feelings, our inquiries, they all coexist together. To find the balance we seek, we must understand how they interact and impact one another.

Experiential: Four Spaces

Set aside 15 to 20 minutes for this experiential. You can do this experiential by either writing each space individually, or by using a four spaces chart that you draw on a piece of paper or white board. (Reminder: You can also download and print a four spaces handout from my website, somacultural liberation.com.)

Take a deep breath. Think of an issue(s) that is impacting your life in some way. This can be a challenging or enthralling experience. Describe how the issue(s) impacts your system in each of the designated spaces: body, mind, emotion, existential. Remember to breathe throughout this experiential.

Take a deep breath. Take 10 minutes and write about what you may have learned about yourself through the four spaces experiential. What spaces were easier for you to work with? Did any themes emerge? What spaces were you challenged by? Do any of the spaces contain more information than the other? What was this experiential like for you?

SUNGLASSES

> And there's just no use because nothing gets to you. I could bleed and you'd still want proof. Help me God I feel so confused. I need some prayer to get me through.
>
> —ROGER KUHN, PHD, *Proof*

People will question your audacity to shine, and even worse, some people will try to steal your shine. Can you relate to being told that you are too much? Many of us have our stories where other people, sometimes people we deeply love, admire, and respect, say something to us that hurts us and makes us want to hide. The sensation of wanting to hide can manifest in many ways. It may be a literal hiding wherein one may leave a situation and return to a physical space where they feel safe and comfortable. It may also manifest somatically in a kind of hyper- or hypovigilance. In my case, I learned to try to make my body smaller so as not to be seen. I round my shoulders forward, hold my head low, tighten my belly, speak with a soft, even tone. I give myself credit for not always doing that. There have been spaces and places in my life where I have always allowed myself to shine. One of those places is when I am performing.

From early childhood, I had a penchant for performing. Growing up on the farm I had a lot of outside space around me where I could get lost in the woods for hours. I spent my time in the woods singing, making up dramatic and funny monologues, and fantasizing about being a rock star. Eventually a few other people noticed my love of performing and encouraged me to sing. My early music teachers, Mr. Hall and Mrs. Brantley, each pulled me aside to tell me they believed I had a special talent for singing. I felt inspired by those words and started to sing more and more. I got pretty good at it and started to audition for musicals, got into those musicals, and sometimes even landed the lead role. My fellow students, and sometimes my friends, were not so kind. I started being told that I had an ego, that I was full of myself, that I was conceited. I did not understand how my expression of pure joy, of sharing music and performing for others, made me egotistical. I never told anyone that I was better than them. I never told anyone they were a bad performer. I did always want to be the best I could be, and sometimes I may have been annoyed if other performers were not taking a scene or a song as seriously as I was, though it wasn't because of ego. I struggled mentally and emotionally for years trying to reconcile the egotistical vain person that some people saw, and the kind, loving, humble, and welcoming person I believed myself to be.

After moving to New York, I realized I was less interested in performing other people's music and more interested in telling my own stories through song. I had also been rejected at a few auditions and realized that I was not cut out for the New York theater scene. I started writing my own music and booking gigs shortly afterward.

At my first professional music gig, a gay man in the audience came up to me after my performance and said I should tone down my gayness. I still remember the look on his face. As he shared his opinion, he pulled his lips back and exposed all of his teeth. He was talking through his teeth and looked like he was in pain. It was hurtful to hear. Another time after a music gig, an audience member whom I had known for many years told me that I was coming across angry in some of my songs, specifically the ones that had anything to do with my Native American identity. I did feel anger in that moment, at the ignorant comment she made about my music, my songwriting, and my racial identity in only a few words.

I've had a few people in my life tell me that I am a difficult person to be friends with because I am too self-confident and intimidating. I've been at workshops where people have come up to me and said they wanted to partner with me, but I was too intimidating to talk to. I cannot tell you the number of times I have been told that I am too much. Writing these words, I recognize that I am holding my breath. Deep exhale. Ouch! I do not like it when people tell me I am too much. What does that even mean?

I remember a conversation I had with my primary sex therapy supervisor, Doug. I was recalling a client interaction that I had experienced a few days prior. I told Doug that it was a first session meeting and that the client had reached out because he was experiencing intermittent erectile challenges. I had done a consultation with him over the phone, and we seemed like a good match. When it was time for the appointment, I went out into the lobby to welcome my client. I remember the sensation of losing my breath when I saw him. I told Doug that the client was so attractive and I had never been attracted to a client like that before. Doug listened to my story for a few minutes, then asked me to pause and take a deep breath. He then said to me, "He's not attractive. YOU are attracted TO him." Wow. My jaw dropped and I noticed my breath tighten in my chest. Then a smile began to spread across my face. "Holy shit, Doug. OMFG!" I am attracted to him. Those were my feelings, and I needed to work through them so that I could best serve the client. In some therapy circles that is called countertransference; I've always called it being human.

I had another aha moment about that clinical interaction. I wanted my client to dim his shine. I wanted him to be less attractive and radiant so that I could do my job and help him with his goal. I was doing to him what others had done to me; I just wasn't saying it out loud. I spent some time in the days leading up to our next session processing my feelings and really owning what was mine. When I next saw my client, his warm smile during our greeting in the lobby felt different. Yes, I still found him to be an attractive person, though I no longer felt attracted to him. This person could shine as brightly as he wanted to, and I would welcome the glow. That clinical interaction was a revolutionary moment in my own personal growth and development as a therapist and as a fellow *Homo sapiens sapiens* walking through this world.

I used that learning moment from Doug and my client to reflect on all the times I felt even a modicum of rejection. With my therapist as witness, I went back to some painful places and processed the story that I had carried for so long and reframed it from what I now believed was true. It was their feelings that made them say all those hurtful things. My shine was too bright for them, and that was their problem.

In seventh grade, I had a teacher named Ms. Mosbey. She was well organized, knew her stuff, and didn't take shit from anybody. Whenever a kid would get sassy with Ms. Mosbey, she would say to them, "Not me, but you." Those words meant a lot to my seventh-grade self. Whenever Ms. Mosbey would say that, at minimum at least once a week, I was amazed she seemed able to brush of someone's insult so easily. I don't ever remember a student fighting back after those words were said—"Not me, but you."

Those words inspired me to think of the ways in which I am no longer going to have other people's thoughts, feelings, or opinions about me dictate how I live my life. I call this epiphany sunglasses.

Ever hear the technique for anxious public speakers—picture the audience naked? Sunglasses is similar in that it is a way to see others. When I enter spaces where I am going to be speaking, performing, or letting my voice be heard, I imagine myself walking up to everyone and offering them a pair of sunglasses. I then tell them, "My intention is to shine, to not dim myself, to glow, to burn until an ember remains, which sparks a flame that burns until my last breath. If my light is too bright for you, I offer you these sunglasses to protect your delicate view. The sun does what the sun does, it shines. I, like the sun, am doing what I am supposed to do, I'm living my life with as much freedom and liberation as I can." Prolific oracle and tarot card deck creator Kim Krans (2019) wrote "Through giving back to people, we become more like the sun itself, radiant, light, and expecting nothing in return" (p. 195). I read these words the morning as I was writing this section. Part of my daily intention practice is to pull an oracle card and see how/or if it resonates with my overall intention or what may be present in my life. Today's card was LIII Splendor Solis/Sun's Splendor, which, according to Krans, is reflective of generosity, health, and abundance. Pulling a card about the sun while writing about my sunglasses practice feels like a synchronous moment in my life. Like the sun, Rog, just do what it is you do—be radiant, and be light, and work on expectations (I'm human after all); let the sunglasses handle the rest.

THE BODY AS WITNESS

My mother was born in rural Alabama. Her mother, Dorothy McGhee Rolin, was full-blood Poarch Creek and her father was a mix of Creek, White, and Black. She lived the first twenty-three years of her life in the same rural Alabama vicinity. By the time she met my father, she had already been married, had two children, escaped domestic violence, and divorced, gaining full custody of her children. My mom tells me how she was desperate to get out of the situations she had experienced in her life during her childhood, from a racist attack on her family involving the KKK, to her father's alcoholism. My mom already had already gone through a lifetime of trauma before she met her first husband who traumatized her, before she met her second husband, my father, who traumatized her, and before she met her third husband who also traumatized her. The thing she desired most, assimilation, was also what continued to cause her pain.

My mom has told me about her assimilation attempts. She has tried to relax her naturally wavy hair. She has dyed her hair a lighter color. She learned specific dances popular in White culture. She dated and then married White men. She did not learn many things about her Creek culture. My mom tells me growing up and being Native in that region of the United States was looked upon in a very negative way. People were shamed for living within the culturally traditional ways of their Muscogee ancestors and Christianity became the dominating assimilation tool.

While married to my father, my mom would take us to weekly Catholic services. She did not identify as Catholic, nor would she participate in most of the in-service rituals (prayers, Communion). She would sing though. Most of the songs were somber at our church, though I always remember singing being the way she would actively participate. Sometimes she would participate in other ways as well. I remember one time, I was likely around six or seven years old, when my mom pulled my belt loop so that I would sit down because I did not sit fast enough after instructed by the priest. She later scolded me and told me not to bring attention to myself at church.

Occasionally, my mom would take my sister Misty and me out for a walk after church. She would tell us that there were other ways to think about God and heaven. She would tell us that we could include animals and nature—plants, trees, water—as some of the ways we could also think about spirit. I have since asked her about these walks. She remembers feeling conflicted about raising my youngest sister and me in a predominately White culture and community. My older sisters spent their early childhood years around my mother's Native family, while my sister Misty, who is three years older, and I spent our childhood years around our father's White family. Mom always told me to identify as Native first and that I should never be ashamed about being Native American. She always spoke with great reverence about her mother and siblings as well as the tribal community as a whole. The struggles with her identity were less about her having shame about her Native American identity and more about the ongoing impact colonization has on Indigenous people. Assimilation is one way out, a supposed promised way, of poverty that was caused by colonization in the first place. It is a vicious cycle that some Indigenous people struggle with. My mother and, certainly, I experience this conflict with our identities because of the cultures in which we were raised.

In the small town of Napoleon, ND, there were many years when my mother was the only non-White person in the community. My father's family, who identified as Americans of German-Russian descent, was not always kind to my mother. According to my paternal grandmother, my mom had several strikes against her. She wasn't White. She wasn't

Catholic. She was divorced. She already had two kids. This became a constant source of contention between my grandmother and my parents. When my grandmother wanted to speak negatively about my mom, she would switch from English to German. I recall many moments throughout my childhood when my grandma would gossip about my mom over the phone to her friends. Although I wasn't fluent in German, because my father often spoke German with his parents and his friends, I was familiar with certain words and phrases. It was also very obvious what was happening when my grandmother would do it.

I believe my mom deals with a lot of intergenerational trauma. Consider that her ancestors were among the first to meet the colonizers, and then her ancestors were forced onto the Trail of Tears or into hiding or assimilation. The trauma within her own home is an example of the impact of colonialism on Indigenous families. Though my mom and her family are Indigenous to what is now called southern Alabama, they were not landowners. Assimilation as a way out of the intergenerational trauma perpetuated many of the issues around Native identity and bodily autonomy that Indigenous people have been experiencing since the 1492 invasion.

I am fortunate to have a good relationship with my mom. Her name is Joyce, by the way. She is a lovely human being. Kind, warm, generous, big auntie energy. She gets along really well with her family. Joyce is currently the matriarch of the Rolin clan. As our family comes from a matrilineal society, my mother is now the oldest female of all her siblings, which makes her the matriarch. It is a role she is growing into as she continues to grieve the loss of her mom and two elder sisters. It is an interesting experience to witness. Because we lived far from my mother's family during my childhood, I have more memories of my mom interacting with my father's family than with her own. My mom currently lives on the Poarch Creek Indians Reservation among her family and fellow tribal members. By the time she returned there, I had already left home and was living in New York City. When I visit my mom, I often spend time with her, my sisters and niece, and my favorite auntie, Deb. Knowing our family clan looks to her for comfort and gentle leadership is in many ways healing because of the cultural significance, but also complicated because of my personal relationship to Joyce, who also happens to be my mother.

I have conflict with my mom, not with Joyce, the matriarch. I believe that parent-child relationships are a culture in and of themselves. There are a lot of supposed tos and shoulds when it comes to a parent-child relationship. Depending on the cultural context, sometimes children (or one of the children) become responsible for the parents after a certain age. In American culture, we are raised to hold reverence and obedience toward our parents. Although this is a relatively broad perspective, certain states allow children under the age of eighteen to seek certain medical interventions such as mental health and sexual health without their parents' consent. This is because there are sometimes differences between a parent's cultural value set and their child's, which brings forth an interesting inquiry: Do parents have the legal authority to determine their child's cultural choices until the age of eighteen? This may include a number of cultural issues such as religion, education, work, and so on.

Joyce and I have quite a few cultural conflicts. We hold different political ideologies on certain issues. We hold different religious and spiritual beliefs. We hold differing opinions on racial issues. We hold different levels of education and access in the world. These issues have not caused harm between us because my mom, who also happens to be a woman named Joyce, is open to hearing my thoughts and opinions. She will often thank me after our conversations because she says she learned something.

When I say these cultural conflicts have not caused an issue between us, I mean I have had to learn how to separate Joyce from the woman who is my mom. This took me many years to process and unpack, and it is an ongoing process. Many times in my life I resented my mom for not doing enough to take care of me. When I was younger, I was incredibly conflicted. I wanted to help my mom escape from the abuses she endured from my father, and I also wanted her to rescue me from my abuse. I wanted her to stand up and fight my dad, kill him if necessary, for what he had done and was doing to all of us. I also wanted to help my mom get out of poverty. I remember coaching her through her GED exam when I was nine years old. She would eventually go on to receive her LPN license. I also was very ashamed of being poor, and I resented my mom for not going to school earlier so we could have a better house and I could have money to take dance classes and voice lessons. I always viewed my mom as being bad with money and thought that my problems with money all came from her because she didn't teach me fiscal responsibility. When I moved to New York City, my mom did help me out financially a few times, one time saving me from eviction. I felt like an asshole the day the money she sent me arrived via Western Union. I had judged her, resented her, held anger toward her for not having money when I was younger, and here she was, probably sending me the last money she had so I could pay my rent. Though I had many wants from my mom, I never had any doubts she loved me.

As an adult, I have been able to reflect upon the idea that my mom gave me my need of being loved, in the best way that Joyce could. Joyce had years of trauma before I came into her life. Joyce continued to experience trauma once I was in her life. But, I saw my mom in a way that Joyce did not see herself. I saw my mom as a strong, independent Indigenous woman who, despite years of trauma, continued to fight for herself and her family. I always believed my mom could do more than she was doing. Joyce continuously thought of herself as not good enough. I was too young to understand how trauma impacts someone's experiences. I certainly had my own traumas, but it wasn't until I was older that I was able to recognize how my traumas impacted who I am and what I know. This knowledge also has to apply to my mom, Joyce, and any other person who has experienced trauma of some kind. With that understanding, I can claim Joyce gave me what I needed, though I still had many wants from my mom.

My mom came to see me in New York a week before my wedding, which was being held in Provincetown, MA. While she was there, we went to see *The Lion King* on Broadway. *The Lion King* is her favorite Disney movie. For the performance, we had seats close to the stage and we were captivated by the opening number. During intermission, she started to cry. I asked her if everything was okay. She told me she was having mixed feelings. She felt joy and excitement at being at the show. She also felt guilt for not supporting me more when I was in musical theater. It was a bittersweet moment between us. I had longed for her approval and support of my decision to be a performer. When I released my album *Proof* in 2006, I was so proud and excited and couldn't wait to share with her. I sent her a copy in the mail, and she said she received it and listened. She told me she enjoyed it. A few years later I was visiting her at her home on the Poarch Creek Indians Reservation and I found the CD unopened among a few other CDs she had lying around in her laundry room. I asked her about it, and she said she would listen to it now. I told her not to bother at this point. I am still not sure if she's ever listened to the album. When I was first published as a contributor in the book *Diverse Bodies, Diverse Practices* (Johnson, 2018), I sent her a copy of the book. She told me she read my chapter, though she didn't understand most of it. She didn't comment on any of the writing that included her and my father. She knows that I am writing this book, and she knows that I will include parts of her story in my writing. She told me she supports me including my perspective of her life and our interactions.

One of the cultural conflicts I have with my mom is her usage of prescription medications to numb her emotional pain. My sisters and I have had numerous conversations about how we can best help our mother overcome her dependency on substances including nicotine, Xanax, and pain pills. I have told her on numerous occasions that I did not want to lose another parent to addiction. It is always a painful conversation to have with her. I do not like to see my mom in any sort of discomfort or pain; this includes somatic, intellectual, emotional, or spiritual. I recognize, understand, and empathize with her choice to use substances as a way to numb her pain. I also see her substance usage from an intergenerational lens. Substances have long been a tool of colonial control. The easy access many Native people have to harmful and addictive substances should come as no surprise as it is an intentional propagation of colonization.

I have talked to my mom about my most recent line of work as a psychotherapist, sex therapist, college professor, and sexuality educator. She has shared how proud of me she is for all that I have accomplished. Since 2021, whenever she sends me something in the mail, she addresses it to Dr. Roger Kuhn. She attended my dissertation defense, which was held over Zoom, even though she often feels challenged by technology. When

I was featured in the 2022 Levi's Pride campaign, she was hospitalized the month the ad was running in Target and Macy stores and was unable to see the display in person. My sister Diva was able to secure the in-store display, however, and my mom now has the display hanging on her wall at her home. I can feel her taking a more active interest in my work, and I believe it is because she has more space to do so. Though she may still feel the impact of the trauma she has experienced in her life, she has told me she recognizes the threats of abandonment and domestic violence are no longer experiences she is dealing with in the present moment. In my forty-six years of life, it is only in the past decade that I have felt the full embrace of Joyce Kuhn as my mom.

My Native identity differs from Joyce's in significant ways. When we consider varying aspects of our positionalities, it becomes clearer. Though we both identify as Poarch Creek, my mom spent the first twenty-seven years of her life among her tribal people, where she currently resides and has been residing for the past thirty years. I spent most of my life away from my tribal people. My mother is known on our homelands because that is her home. I am known there because of my mother and my relationships to her family. I have studied and now teach American Indian studies at college. My mom has never taken an American Indian studies class and does not know much about the history or legal issues from a broader Native perspective. My mom has helped me find my identity as a Poarch Creek person and my mom has told me that I have helped her better understand her identity as Native American.

Because of my close relationship with my mom, and my desire for her to know and understand more about my work, I invited her to participate in a BOLD ADDRESSING assessment. My mom is one of only a handful of people I have done a BOLD ADDRESSING assessment with who, when it comes to O for occupy, can lay claim to living on, not occupying, the land of her ancestors. When she talks about living in her homelands I feel a deep sense of pride emanating from her.

* * *

My mom's relationship to her body is an incredibly interesting topic. I am thankful that we had an opportunity to discuss this relationship because I learned that she sees my body as an extension of hers. Though she fully understands I am a separate and independent entity, she sees herself as my life-giver and thus I am a part of her body. She's not wrong. I've always known that to be factual, though I didn't reflect on the meaning that had to my mom until I asked her about her relationship to her body. I also learned more about how racial dynamics impacted the way she felt among my father's family and what it was like for her to be a small-framed Indigenous woman working in a White male–dominated assembly line for a major agricultural company. When I asked her about L for lived experience, she became animated and said she identifies as a mother, grandmother, sister, daughter, and nurse. I remember her smiling as she shared, and a tear rolled down her cheek. She said she was happy thinking about her family. She shared she wants to be remembered most by her love for her family.

My mom is at the age, seventy-four, where she recognizes she must get certain things in order as she transitions to her later elder years. She has had conversations with all her children about what her wishes are when she transitions to be with the ancestors. I feel too young to be having these conversations. I feel not ready to have these conversations. Yet, they remain necessary because they too represent a specific faction of culture. Depending on cultural beliefs and thus cultural conflicts, whenever two or more people are involved, it is always beneficial to be as clear as possible in order for everyone to understand, collaborate if necessary, and move toward collective goals. I understand and recognize that we often do not have time to share BOLD ADDRESSING assessments with one another to understand each other's positionality better. I will continue to suggest we learn as much about ourselves as we can so that we are best equipped to understand any reactions, questions, or curiosities we may have in relations to others.

Questions remain about who Joyce Kuhn is. I have a better understanding thanks to her participating in a BOLD ADDRESSING assessment with me, though of course this assessment is just one way of inquiring about one's positionality and epistemology. I will never know my mom the way her friends know her. This astonished me until I recently had a similar realization about my friend Alexis and her three children. Though I have known her children since they were born, I knew their mom fifteen years earlier in our formative early twenties in New York City. They will never know their mom in a way that I do, and how could they? We all have different experiences with the same person. To me she is Alexis; to them she is mom. I believe that I know Joyce as my mom, because that is who and what she is to me, in addition to as a friend because I also consider my mom one of my best friends. Though Joyce is, among many things, a mother, she is my mother, thus making her unique and extra special to me. To others, though, she is Joyce and exists in a more autonomous way than motherhood allows. These intersections of identity and the cultural implications attached to them are relevant in understanding the beauty and the complexity of the human experience. What does it mean to know someone anyway? What are the cultural markers of knowing someone?

Part of the ways I am healing from the trauma I experienced with my father is by applying the same lens to him as I have to my mom. I understand that my father was also a person named Gary. Gary had his own experiences, traumas, and cultural conflicts with the world around him. Gary made choices in his life that resulted in me being born. Gary wasn't prepared for his youngest child, and only male child in the family, to have a darker skin color and darker eyes than he had. Gary did not want a child who looked like an Indian. Gary did not want a male child who seemed feminine to himself and others. I was that child, and Gary was my father. Those intersections exist on individual and interpersonal levels. Since my father is deceased, I am not able to do a full BOLD ADDRESSING assessment with him since the assessment is meant to be an interactive process of self-reflection and sharing by the person taking the assessment. Anyone can apply a BOLD ADDRESSING assessment to someone who is deceased, though they would likely be filling in a lot of information via research (if available), rather than by hearing from the person directly. Though my work has only focused on using a BOLD ADDRESSING assessment as part of a somacultural liberatory format with living people, I am certainly interested in what it may be like to use the assessment to reflect upon our past.

I did not have a good relationship with my father. I spoke to him a week prior to his death, though only because it was his fiftieth birthday.

He created a culture of secrecy in our home around his drinking, his selling drugs, and the abuse he inflicted upon his family. I never told him that I was gay. I never told him that I feared him. Though my father was known as the town drunk in our little farming community, no one seemed to be all that concerned about the people living in the home with the town drunk. I was twenty-three when my father died from a drunk driving accident. The sheriff believes he may have hit an ice patch when swerving to miss a deer. He wasn't wearing a seat belt. Thankfully, he was alone and no one else was injured. The accident happened after midnight in mid-November in rural North Dakota. The accident wasn't discovered until a few hours later.

A large part of my early narrative is shaped by my positionality in having an abusive alcoholic father as a parent. I lived in a hypervigilant state around my father almost the entire time I knew him. Though I have occasional fond memories of my father, most of my memories constrict my system and make me hold my breath. Most of the time when I think about my father, I feel a bracing in my system. Even as I write these words, I am noticing a tightness in my chest and in my throat. Like my mom, like Joyce, I too need to be reminded that Gary Kuhn is no longer around. He can no longer physically hurt any of us, or anyone, ever again.

Emphasis here on physical. From an intellectual, emotional, and existential perspective, I continue to work through some of the trauma I experienced involving my father. I do drink alcohol and have been drunk too many times in my life to count. I do not believe that I have ever had an issue with abusing alcohol, and still alcohol can be a big trigger for me. I do not like to be around other people who are drunk if I am not drinking. I especially dislike being around my partner if he has been drinking and I have not. It is not the way that my partner behaves, which is usually silly when he is drinking; it is what being around someone who is drunk when I am not represents in my life. I have explained this to my husband, Sean, and he is very cognizant of making sure that it rarely happens. I know it is a defense, and understanding where the defense comes from and the impact it has on my life has been incredibly helpful. I am able to recognize what my issues are with alcohol and that other people do not have similar issues around alcohol use, abuse, or disuse. This also applies to my father.

Centering myself in the work that I do is of interest to me from a somacultural perspective because my life is the greatest reference I have to this theory; this will be true for you as well. We know our stories better than anyone else. If we are willing, we can begin to understand the impact culture has and will continue to play in our bodily sensations, movements, and behaviors. I have previously written about challenges I experience having been raised in a biracial and bicultural home (Johnson, 2018). My parents wanted me to identify not as biracial, rather as one over the other. My mom would tell me to always identify as Native and to be proud of being Poarch Creek. My dad would tell me that I should always tell people that I was German-Russian and to be proud of my strong German name. Despite being married to a Native American woman and having a best friend who was also Native American, my father was an incredibly racist person who valued American imperialism over his Native wife and children.

To understand my father is to understand aspects of his positionality. He was a child of the 1950s and grew up watching John Wayne movies and TV westerns that had a heavy focus on cowboys versus Indians. He cast himself in the role of the hero cowboy and got himself a Native woman as a status symbol. It does not feel good to write these things about my father, though I do believe them to be true. He did not mind that his wife was not White. His children needed to be White though. He found many negative things about me including my sexuality and my being an additional race than him. He desired to rid me of my Native identity and to literally straighten me out.

As I desperately wanted to leave North Dakota, I took my father up on an offer he made me the summer after my junior year of high school. Instead of going to the performing arts school that I had attended for the past three summers, I would live on the farm with him and learn to do various tasks including welding, changing oil in a vehicle, changing tires, and operating a large tractor. The last time I had been on a tractor was the night he had beaten me so severely that my parents separated. Needing the money, I said yes against everything my body was telling me. The summer, as my body had predicted, was a disaster. The only silver lining was reconnecting with some of my childhood friends who still lived in

Napoleon, including James and Cleo. The summer I turned sixteen was the summer that would forever change my relationship to my father, to my childhood that haunted me.

In a drunken rage one night that summer, my father burst into the room I had turned into my bedroom (the former room of my older sisters, Tammy and Diva) and demanded that I go for a walk with him. He took me around the farm and showed me various marijuana plants that he was growing and dehydrating, preparing to sell them. He also told me about his sexual indiscretions throughout his life and in particular during his marriage to my mom. When he passed out a few hours later, I packed everything up in my car and left. I didn't leave town immediately. Instead, I drove through the small farming town, reminiscing about my childhood and how toxic and damaging it was. I drove past my paternal grandmother's home and shed a tear about her passing. I drove past my childhood best friend's house, James, and waved goodbye knowing it was too early to try to say goodbye in person. I drove past my former elementary school and parked outside for a few moments. I said goodbye to my former self and left town from there. I took the back country roads, a route my father had shown me earlier that summer. I screamed and cried and sang at the top of my lungs. I did not return to the farm until my father's funeral. After his death, my sisters and I opted to sell the farm to my aunt Bonnie. She and her husband tore down all of the buildings, and the property is now used as farm land; good riddance.

I've been back to Napoleon one time since my father's death. I took my husband, Sean, there to see the town. We drove to the old farm, and it was a revelation to see the buildings no longer standing. I did visit the cemetery where my father is buried. Though I did pass by his grave, I was there to pay respects to my grandmother, whom I loved despite her ignorant behavior toward my mother.

Though my father is a key player in the narrative of my early years, I consciously choose not to focus on him in my current life. His death relatively early in my adulthood made this an easy shift as I do not have new stories involving him that disrupt my life. The only new memory I have of my father came from a dream I experienced about a decade after his death. I was reading a book about lucid dreaming and one of the assignments was to invite your nightmare character (if you had one) into your dream through a lucid dream state. Since my early childhood, I had nightmares involving the character Regan from the film *The Exorcist*. I knew Regan was who I needed to invite into my lucid dream. When I did have the lucid dream about Regan, I demanded she take off her mask and reveal her true identity. Underneath the Regan mask was the face of my father. It made perfect sense to me that Regan was a symbol of my father. Since that night, now over a decade ago, I have not had another dream about Regan. I did once have a vision of her during a breathwork session, though. She was dancing along a cliff near the ocean. She seemed happy. I did not fear her like I had in the past. She, like my father, was also dead.

ROGER J. KUHN, PHD

The two greatest areas of shame in my life are not around my sexuality or my racial identity. My two greatest areas of shame are poverty and lack of education. The irony of these being my shame triggers is they are no longer real issues of concern in my life. I no longer live in poverty, and I went through enough schooling to obtain a doctoral degree. Yet, my perpetual habit of saying yes to opportunities is based upon the shame and trauma I experienced while living in poverty. My experience with education is similar. Because I did not take what the dominant US culture would call the traditional route and go to college immediately after high school, I always felt judged and limited to what I would be able to obtain professionally, which would thus leave me in an endless cycle of poverty.

Poverty and lack of education are intricately linked in North America. Black, Indigenous, and People of Color (BIPOC) communities throughout the continent have been subjected to policies that seek to misinform and withhold valuable and potentially lifesaving information. By gaining voting rights and access to education and financial institutions, BIPOC people and communities have tried to bring a greater sense of equity and equality to their lives in relation to those of their oppressors. Policies such as affirmative action for BIPOC in college acceptance had been enacted to help mitigate the chasm between an institution that once thrived on differentiating races and giving access to only those deemed worthy—White males. The link between poverty and education does not begin at the university or college level; rather, policies were created that made access to education a challenge, thus continuing a cycle of poverty for many BIPOC people.

An example is the differentiation between the education Poarch Creek children received and the education that children in the Alabama public school system received prior to 1947. In the 1940s Poarch Creek children attended an Indian school that only went through sixth grade. The public school bus would not stop to pick up older Poarch Creek children, thus making it extremely challenging and sometimes impossible for Native children to go to school beyond that point, thus potentially relegating them to a life of poverty. One of the stories that forever changed the history of the Poarch Creek people is that of Jack Daughtry. Jack was a Poarch Creek member who wanted his daughters Earline and Pearline to be able to attend the public school and continue their education. Since the bus would not stop for his children, or any other Native children, one day in 1947, Jack Daughtry stood in front of the school bus until the bus driver allowed his children and other Poarch Creek children to get on the bus and go to school. His one act inspired the former Chief of the Poarch Creek nation, Calvin McGhee, to bring a lawsuit against the county school board. Their efforts ensured, at a minimum, access to public education for all Poarch Creek children aged beyond the Indian school's limitation of sixth grade.

Years later, as the Poarch Creek nation itself grew out of poverty, thanks in part to investments made in casinos and manufacturing contracts with the US government, scholarships were made available to all tribal members to be used toward pursuing education. The funds could be used to help pay for private school for tribal members under the age of eighteen. Funds could be used for certifications, as well as for college degrees. When these funds became available, I was already pursuing healing from my education shame, which for me meant that I was working toward my associate's degree. Once the scholarship became available, I decided that my pursuit of education would be an homage to my ancestors who did not have the same opportunities as I did, and a vessel for breaking the intergeneration cycles of poverty that complicated the lives of my maternal family members.

I felt the shame evoked by my lack of higher education somatically. As I was going through the process of obtaining my degrees, I noticed the shame felt different in my body with each degree I earned and accumulated. I resonate with the idea that comparison is the thief of joy. Throughout my higher education journey, I often compared myself to others who had a higher degree than I did. The shame would magnify if I learned the person was younger than I was. The intersections mattered because I placed cultural relevance on the intersections; young and higher educated, earning a lot of income and having higher education, and so on; the list of intersection comparisons alone could easily take up a chapter in this book. Again, if I focus on only the story, I can over-intellectualize and potentially miss or unconsciously ignore the somatic and/or emotional experience that I may also be having. I may miss the behavioral adaptation that my system makes to feel the sensation and feeling of shame. Are you aware of any behavioral adaptations that you may make when you experience the sensations and feelings of shame?

One of the behavioral adaptations that I made in healing my educational shame was to prioritize education as a value. This required me to spend many nights and weekends doing schoolwork, which left little time for socializing and pursuing other goals and passions. The more I prioritized education as a top-five value, the more I naturally began to create space in my life to accomplish my educational goals. Although it was not always easy, and I became very annoyed with myself at times, I am proud that I honored my commitment to the value of education. It helped me remove some of the stigma I had associated with not having obtained my college degree at an earlier point in my life. I felt an end to the prioritization of education as a top-five value the moment it was announced that I passed my dissertation and had earned the title doctor of philosophy. The following morning, I gave a presentation at 7 a.m. PST to approximately 120 people on the topic of love and community healing. During my introduction, I made a joke that the workshop participants could call me doctor now. I remember coughing a bit, and a zap of energy coursed through my body. I continued on and had a fantastic time with the participants. Afterward, I realized something felt different in my system. A familiar heaviness in my body was gone. Throughout that day, I received texts and social media posts congratulating me on achieving my doctoral degree. I felt really seen that day. I also realized most of the people who were writing me or calling me were unaware of the shame I carried regarding my lack of education. I had done a really great job of not showing signs of any challenges I had around the topic. I had become really good at constricting my body in order to not feel somatic and emotional feelings that are present when I experience shame.

My intention in including information about my education journey has many purposes. First, there is the cultural consideration that includes the colonial attempt to suppress Native education. Second, there is the vulnerability aspect of sharing something that feels incredibly personal to me in the hopes that someone may relate and possibly become inspired by my determination to acquire a higher education degree. Third, there is the recognition that even though we can experience something in a less impactful way, it does not mean that the trigger is gone entirely. Fourth, I believe my educational path and my relationship to this path are good examples of a somacultural framework. Because I understood the reasoning behind my passion and dedication to pursuing higher education and the impact it had on my bodily experiences, I was able to approach the process in a more direct way that was about me and not about societal and cultural expectations.

Even though I have a PhD, I still find I am somewhat triggered by talking about my once lack of a higher education degree. I recognize that, for over twenty years, I conditioned my body to a very specific somatic reaction, which has created a constrictive reflex. When I am aware that I am constricting due to feeling triggered about education, I need only take a deep breath and remind myself what is true in the moment, and I can begin to relax again. Connecting with my breath is one of the ways that I have found useful in keeping my body more regulated. Things that I find evocative or triggering impact me in different ways. Some issues I have a new relationship with, and they bother me less. Some issues I have been experiencing for as long as I can remember, and they can range on a scale anywhere from mildly annoying to panic inducing. Knowing what my system finds evocative and the impact(s) the triggering experience has on my system has enabled me to be better equipped to respond to a trigger in a way that keeps me more powerfully aligned with regulation.

Often I am asked about how someone can understand what issues in life they find evocative to the point of dysregulation. Although there is not one steadfast solution to this inquiry, I generally respond by asking people two questions: Are you able to sense when you are angry about something? Does this feeling of anger create any sensations in your body? I ask questions about anger because it is often a visceral experience that people can feel into. One could ask these questions with several emotional experiences: happiness, sadness, nervousness, and so on. I chose anger because it is the emotion for which I learned how to locate emotion-based sensations in my body. I often feel what I call a quiet rage coursing through my system. This feeling is in part due to trauma I have experienced and also because of the injustice I see in the world on a constant basis. I know that I am not alone in my quiet rage, though sometimes I also feel very isolated in these feelings, which can create a compounding effect on my system. When I ask questions about feeling an emotion and then sensing the somatic reaction, I am often met with a "yes and yes" response. When someone answers "yes and yes," I tell them since they are able to recognize when they feel anger and are able to locate how the feelings of anger sometimes react in their system, the inquiry then becomes about learning what the causes of the anger they experience may be. When I ask people what makes them angry, they will often tell a story about a time they felt really angry. I believe stories are so incredibly important in helping us understand situations. I also believe we can get stuck in our stories and are unable to let them go because we have unresolved somatic, intellectual, emotional, and existential inquiries about them. Some stories last for years, and others drift into the far corners of our consciousness and memory. What is always important about story in our lives is the emotional experience generated by the story. The emotions we experience in our personal and collective stories are linked to the values that we hold in our lives. When we can name the value that is attached to the emotional experience, we can then understand how this value shows up again and again in the moment when we feel triggered. If I value kindness and someone is intentionally rude to me, I will no doubt be hurt and angered by what they said. I may notice my chest feels like it is on fire and my heart rate is accelerating. I may even say something unkind back to them, and when I do, I will undoubtedly feel an immense sense of guilt and shame. I did not feel my value of kindness being honored, nor did I honor it myself. The story is important, and the emotional and somatic response based upon the value(s) being impacted is where I believe the work is. The work I refer to here is our growth-work—the work we do in order to feel more aligned with ourselves and the work we do in order to stay closer to homeostasis, our most balanced and regulated state.

Upon any intake I do for my psychotherapy and sex therapy practice, I inform new clients that I am open to hearing whatever they would like to share. I also qualify this by explaining the four mandatory instances when I am required to breach confidentiality in the state of California—if you disclose that a child, an elder, or a dependent adult is in some way being harmed, or if you yourself are planning to cause physical injury to someone (rape, murder). I also add, though it is not legally required, it is legally permitted to break confidentiality around suicidal ideation. I take suicidal ideation very seriously in my practice and inform clients that should they tell me about a plan for a suicide attempt, I will put a plan into motion to get them immediate psychiatric services. Once this crucial information is shared during the intake process, I always say the following line to people, "With all that being said, whatever might be on your mind—sex, drugs, rock and roll—is welcome here." I also tell clients they can share what they like, though it is not necessary to share details. I tell clients "The important thing (and why I believe you reached out to me) is that you are having some kind of somatic, intellectual, emotional, or existential challenge with whatever it is that you are experiencing." Understanding the impacts on our system and the somatic, intellectual, emotional, and existential feelings that arise from these impacts is the foundation of somacultural liberation.

Experiential: Growth Work

Take a moment and reflect upon areas in your life where you may experience shame. Use your BOLD ADDRESSING assessment as a helpful reminder of the varying aspects of your identity. Write and reflect upon any intersections within your positionality that may impact feelings of shame. What cultural meaning or significance have you given this issue regarding the intersections of your identity and the impact that it has on your overall regulation? Is there anything that might make these feelings of shame less? What might you be willing to do to shift your relationship to the impact shame has on your body, mind, and spirit?

LIBERATION MODALITIES

I do not have a specific recommendation in terms of a somatic modality that best fits within the somacultural framework. I do not believe in a hierarchy of somatic modalities because each body and everybody is different and unique. What works for me may work for you, or you may prefer to do something different. Somatic modalities can include meditating, exercising, crafting, star gazing, gardening, having sex, cooking, laughing, crying, or using a punching bag to release emotion. There are also several branded somatic modalities including Somatic Experiencing, Generative Somatics, Breema, the 5Rhythms, and The Wheel of Consent. I am choosing to focus on the latter two, as those are the modalities that most resonate with my system and how I want to be seen in the world.

The 5Rhythms is a movement- and dance-based modality that was created by Gabrielle Roth. Gabrielle believed there were five rhythms that were accessible to us at any given moment in time: flowing, staccato, chaos, lyrical, and stillness. Flowing is Gabrielle's way of describing feminine energy—soft, circular, grounded. Staccato is her way of describing masculine energy—sharp, linear, direct. Chaos is the point where the feminine and the masculine meet—high energy, release, surrender. Lyrical is the rhythm that signifies coming through the chaos—light, floating, easeful. Finally, stillness represents acceptance, attunement with the body, with spirit, with source. Dancing the rhythms gave me a sense of comfort in my body. I could dance with my joy, my pain, my sorrow, my eroticism. There were no wrong steps or choreography to follow. The 5Rhythms were not about how Gabrielle thought my body should move, rather about how my body wanted to move. The rhythms were a revelation and I credit Gabrielle and the entire 5Rhythms community for inspiring the early foundations of my work around somacultural liberation. Apart from singing and sex, I feel most connected to my body and my spirit when I am dancing. My friend Shani, whom I introduced 5Rhythms to, shared that taking a class was like going to church, the gym, and an amazing discotheque all in one. She is absolutely right.

I was introduced to the 5Rhythms in my mid-twenties by a friend, Meyoung, who informed me that I would not regret taking the class. She was correct, and after the first class, I embarked on a quest to understand my pleasure and my pain through this modality. The 5Rhythms were my main source of somacultural liberation throughout my twenties and into my early thirties. I took a class a minimum of once weekly and often twice a week. I also took workshops, read all of Gabrielle's books, and listened to her music. I also became part of the crew, helping set up and dismantle the weekly classes that were held in New York City. Being a part of the crew gave me access to the teachers, including Gabrielle, who always embraced me and made me feel like a welcome member of the community. I write more about my journey with the 5Rhythms in my contribution, "Fieldwork," to the incredible book *Diverse Bodies, Diverse Practices* (Johnson, 2018). I highly recommend checking out her book *Sweat Your Prayers* (1997), and if you have the opportunity, taking a 5Rhythms class, which you can find across the globe led by a variety of fantastic teachers.

THE WHEEL OF CONSENT

As previously mentioned, when discussing somacultural liberation, it is necessary to talk about uncomfortable topics. Genocide, slavery, misogyny, homophobia, racism, xenophobia, and the like are rooted in nonconsensual ideations. Consent is an ideology and a practice that is rooted in clear, undisputed agreements for something to happen, or for something to be done for self and/or others. We live in a world where consent is not only devalued but also incredibly misunderstood. In order to move toward a liberation framework, I believe we must center ourselves and our work in consent. Yes, this can be incredibly difficult to do, primarily because to talk about uncomfortable topics requires the consent of those you are talking to. Imagine a world where we asked one another if we could express our pain and discomfort with an idea or practice. Imagine if we all were asked if it was okay for us to have our rights taken away from us or if a law could be imposed that threatened our safety. Naysayers may argue that this is what voting is for. Sure, voting can help bring some beneficial results, but ask a minority how they feel about the majority deciding how they should live their life. We should never live in a system that awards the majority the right to decide how a minority culture lives (unless, of course, that minority culture intends to do harm to others). There can be no true liberation if majorities exercise their positionality, privilege, and power to hinder the freedom of others.

Consent ideology tends to focus on self in relation to another or others. I suggest we also talk about consent with self. Are the choices we make truly our own, or are we pressured into doing certain things, in a certain way, in order to please others? According to the work of Betty Martin (Martin & Dalzen, 2021), people pleasers are living nonconsensually because consent requires clear, undisputed agreements. If you are or I am doing something to appease someone else at the expense of ourselves, we are people pleasing, which leads to all kinds of complications. People pleasing is not always a conscious choice. Rather, people pleasing can be seen and understood to be a defense mechanism that some people employ to be safe. I have no idea how many times I have people pleased throughout my life when someone has inquired about my identity. I have listened to countless people tell me about their distant relative who was Native and how much they love Native culture even though they themselves have never lived as Native, supported Native people, or bothered to understand Native culture. I do not care. I do not care that your great, great, great-grandparent was rumored to be Native. I do not care that you love Native culture and that you have been to a powwow. I do not care that you think Native people are exotic. In the past, I have always listened, nodded my head, smiled, and said, "Wow, thanks for sharing." These days, if someone comes up to me in an unsolicited manner to discuss their family lore around Native identity, I pause them and say, "I am not interested in learning about your family lore. Though if you wish to tell me how you, personally, are helping Native people, then by all means feel free to share." I've pissed off quite a few people saying this, and I still don't care. I do not give my consent to hearing someone talk about family rumors about Native identity. I recognize people do this because they desire to be seen as an ally, though from my perspective, someone isn't a distant Native; either you identify as Native, or you do not. I am not talking about blood quotients or enrollment, as those are colonial tools of oppression. I also do not believe that to be Native you have to have some kind of trauma (outside of colonialism) that you have endured or are enduring, though every Native person I know has survived trauma of some kind. If you, dear reader, come from family lore of Native identity, please do not discuss this with Native people. Do your work to discover if this is true about your family. Understand the reason and choices your family made in order to devalue this part of your identity. Likely you will find it was nonconsensual and the choice was made in order to survive in a brutally racist world.

During my graduate studies in somatic psychology, I was surprised that we were not required to take a course on human sexuality. I was also surprised the subject of sex was not explicitly addressed in my couples counseling course, which was required for graduation and state licensure. I opted to take a one-credit elective in human sexuality and, as previously discussed, went on to obtain my PhD in human sexuality with a concentration in clinical practice. During my doctoral studies, I learned about sensate focus, a touch-based modality created by Masters and Johnson in the 1960s to improve intimacy and communication between partners. I never fully resonated with the practice and neither did my clients, with many telling me they found it boring, confusing, and challenging. Thankfully, I was introduced to the 3-Minute Game by a colleague who shared it was her preferred method of intervention for couples.

The 3-Minute Game was created by Harry Faddis. It is a touch-based modality wherein one partner asks another "How would you like me to touch you for 3 minutes?" After 3 minutes, the person being touched asks, "How would you like to touch me for 3 minutes?" These simple phrases are based upon consent. Betty Martin expanded upon the 3-Minute Game in her Wheel of Consent and offered two specific suggestions: "may I" and "will you." You can find a link to Betty Martin's work on my website.

WHAT DOES IT MEAN TO FEEL LIBERATED IN OUR BODIES?

I recognize many of the questions I ask in this book can only be answered from a subjective experience. I also recognize some may feel disappointed I am not giving "the" answer, while others will feel a sense of excitement, realizing that they can define these terms for themselves. In my work as a psychotherapist, my clients fall into one of these two categories: some who want me to have the answer to the conundrums they are experiencing in their lives will spend years in therapy; others who want me to share the answer may leave out of frustration that the so-called expert in the room isn't an expert at all. To be fair, I am not an expert at anyone's life, not even my own. I am in a constant state of curiosity and exploration, which makes defining terms such as somacultural liberation possible, in that moment. In my experience, clients who understand it is their choice to define terms and experiences in their lives generally fare better in my clinical practice. They bring an excitement and energy to sessions with them. They drop into experientials and can recognize sensations in their body, and they can express what those sensations mean to them.

Is that what it means to be liberated in our body—to recognize, name, and make meaning of sensations? For me, the answer is yes. I do not define a liberated somatic experience as one in which I am only experiencing joy or happiness. Rather, I define it as welcoming whatever sensation may be present in my body—pain, excitement, arousal, hunger, fear, ecstasy. This is not an easy feat. I do not have to like the sensation I am experiencing, though I believe I do need to be with it and not ignore it or try to force my body to feel any other way than what it feels in the moment.

Although I do not experience feelings of depression very often, I have learned to recognize the somatic sensations that feeling depressed awakens in my body. I feel tired, heavy, and clumsy when I am depressed. If I lean into these sensations and move with them, instead of through them, my depressive symptoms transform at a much higher rate. If I stay constricted and try to avoid the sensations, in addition to the heaviness my body feels, I will also feel tightness and heat, which I recognize as the sensations I experience when I am feeling anxious. Ugh! Anxiety and depression at the same time are absolutely dreadful in my experience. Slowing down and being with and moving with the sensations are ways in which I have learned how to bring my system closer to the state of balance that I am (and likely you are) seeking.

Ultimately, I do not believe that we have to be able to define sensations and experiences in clear and concise terms. Saying "I feel tingly" is as valid as saying "I feel a sense of heat and a pulsation that I can only define as lightning coursing through my system." The depth of the definition or the description is not what you need to focus on. Focus on naming the sensation to begin with, and if desired (over time), you may feel the desire to have a more descriptive way of engaging with sensations in your body. The idea here is to get out of your head, and if words, definitions, and descriptions do not come easily for you, don't bother with them. Again, focus on the simplicity of the sensation: heat, cold, tingly, sharp, tight, open, constricted, and so on.

I believe naming something can give and take away power. Many of our aha moments in life come from being able to name what it is we are experiencing. Though I am not keen on making mental health diagnoses in my practice, I recognize the validity of clients wanting to be able to name what they have been experiencing. The *Diagnostic and Statistics Manual of Mental Disorders* (known as the DSM), now in its fifth iteration, is the primary system used by mental health clinicians to diagnose their clients. In the DSM, you will find relatively mundane diagnoses such as adjustment disorder to overtly complicated diagnoses such as schizoaffective disorder. The DSM also operates on a hierarchical nature, with the aforementioned adjustment disorder being the lowest on the rung of the ladder. If, for insurance purposes, a client needs a diagnosis (another reason the insurance system in the US is terrible), adjustment disorder is where all of my clients start because I understand everyone is adjusting to something. Additionally, in my work as a sex therapist, although I know there are diagnostic codes for particular sexual health issues impacting mental health, I refuse to use the DSM codes for erectile disorder or female orgasmic disorder. My client's sexual health is none of the insurance companies' business. Sex is already taboo in the broad culture we associate with the US, and I will always rally against further stigmatizing the people I have the pleasure to assist in the journey toward greater sexual health and fulfillment.

I will, however, talk to clients about the DSM and about the particular diagnosis under which the experience they are having may fall. Naming the challenge and legally diagnosing the challenge are very different things, and each has its own cultural implication that can impact the body. Ask yourself if you would rather carry a diagnosis of adjustment disorder, or a diagnosis of female sexual interest/arousal disorder, or male hypoactive sexual desire disorder. Does one of the diagnoses land better in your system? Can you lean into and breathe into one of the diagnoses more easily? If so, what is that about for you? If you chose adjustment disorder as the easier diagnosis to lean and breathe into, ask yourself, "What is my relationship to hierarchical mental health diagnoses and where did I learn this particular thought process?"

Many people (including some mental health clinicians like myself) will argue the DSM perpetuates harm and systemically marginalizes people who have historically suffered the most due to the racist and homophobic history of the American Psychological Association (APA). Homosexuality as a mental health diagnosis existed for years until it was removed from the DSM in its third iteration in 1974 (two years before my birth). Although there has never been a specific diagnosis for a particular racial category, mental health diagnoses that exist on the diagnosis hierarchy have been used to harm and institutionalize BIPOC throughout the manual's history. Women and trans people have also been (and arguably continue to be) marginalized by the DSM. All of these examples offer proof that the DSM does not understand or consider culture when broadly labeling someone's experience.

Although diagnostic categories such as generalized anxiety disorder, panic disorder, and major depressive disorder may account for any number of traumatic experiences someone may have experienced, there is only one specific category for trauma—posttraumatic stress disorder. Writer, activist, and scholar Andrew Jolivétte (2016) believes there should be a category that implicitly names colonialism as a contributing factor for the ongoing mental and physical health issues BIPOC people experience; he has named this *Post Traumatic Invasion Syndrome*. Jolivétte's perspective is akin to the work of Joy Degruy (2005) who coined the term

Post Traumatic Slave Syndrome as a way to signify the role slavery has played in the mental and physical health of Black people in the United States. The likelihood of these terms making it into the next iteration of the DSM is next to zero, though I truly hope I am wrong.

I find it incredibly curious that there is a diagnosis in the DSM called fetishistic disorder, whereas no diagnosis exists for racism or homophobia. Does the DSM not believe racism and homophobia are mental health disorders though a fetish is? I believe the DSM is unwilling to ever name racism and homophobia as mental health issues because the APA would then need to reconcile their racist and homophobic past with the populations that have been harmed. One of the interesting things about culture is that it is created. We have created a culture around certain issues and conditions that we (meaning those in power to make any real changes) deem mental health issues, while issues, such as racism and homophobia, that actually cause real harm are not considered mental health conditions. I hope we can change this. I'll start right now; racism and homophobia are mental health illnesses. Are we sick?

LIMITATIONS VERSUS BOUNDARIES

As an English speaker born and raised in the lands we now call the United States, I have noticed a cultural phenomenon of using a lot of synonyms in our language system. We use words interchangeably, which may have similar, though slightly different, meanings. A good example of this is *boundaries* versus *limitations* and *needs* versus *wants*.

Let's start by understanding how I differentiate boundaries and limitations. I think of *boundaries* as the relationships we have with ourselves and with others. Examples of relationship with self can include all kinds of experiences such as sex, work, food, health, consumption of media, and spirituality. Examples of relationship with others include family, partners, friends, coworkers, and strangers. *Limitations* are the experiences we have within these boundaries.

Using myself as an example, I believe I exist within a boundary of self. I choose to create boundaries with others and define these boundaries with particular words that have cultural value and significance such as *husband*, *mother*, *father*, *sibling*, *best friend*, *friend*, and *stranger*. My boundary of self does not change; what changes are the limitations within my boundary. My relationship to food and disorganized eating is a good example of this. I understand my body (my boundary) does not fare well with all kinds of food. Although I love spicy foods, I will often feel unwell if I eat too much of this type of food. I have to limit my intake of spicy foods in order to stay with consent within my boundary of self. I know spicy foods are not good for my digestive system (I had my gallbladder removed in my early twenties), and I know that eating spicy foods beyond my limit will be disruptive. It sucks, but living within and knowing my limits have helped me to maintain a greater sense of balance within my system. More balance means a greater sense of happiness. I choose to honor my limitations because I believe happiness is the best spice of life.

I'll take this deeper using my relationship with my husband as an example. I consider my marriage a boundary that defines my relationship to myself, to him, and to others. Within our marriage we have limitations that include how we engage with each other and with others. Although I may lead a rather extroverted life, I am, at my truest self, an introvert. I crave solitude, and after spending large amounts of time with my husband, I begin to feel the need to be alone for a few hours, or a day, in order to recharge my battery. Over the years, we have come to understand that too much time together is a limitation within our relationship for me. Another limitation within the boundary of our relationship is sex outside of our marriage, which is a common limit within many marriages and romantic relationships. Our limit, however, is not no sex outside of the marriage. Our limit is no sex without the other. We have a play-together-to-stay-together limitation and it works for us.

In my clinical work, I have helped many couples renegotiate the limits within the boundary of their relationship. I most often renegotiate limits around sex, which might include sex outside of the marriage, frequency of sex, or the kinds of sexual behaviors and experiences the couple wants to have. Emphasis here on *want*, not *need*, which we will get to in just a moment. Couples often seek my help as a sex therapist because they experience something we refer to in the field as desire discrepancy. Sex outside of the marriage is a kind of desire discrepancy and can be an exhilarating or harrowing experience for a couple. When couples ask me to help them open their marriage, the work involves understanding the limitations within the boundary of their relationship. We do this by a process I call open relationship collaboration. *Collaboration* is a process of being in consent with one another, whereas *compromise* may be a consent violation within self and other regarding limitations within the relational dynamic.

NEEDS VERSUS WANTS

I believe semantics are important. The language that we use on a daily basis can result in joyous or deleterious perspectives on how we value our lives. When we understand the difference between a need and a want, it helps us establish our center of authenticity. Think of a *need* as an experience, feeling, or emotion that you must have to function (i.e., safety, stable job, trust, etc.). Think of a *want* as an experience, feeling, or emotion that would enhance your life, though without it, you would ultimately be okay.

When working with clients, I often use my own life experience to explain the concept of needs versus wants. When I decided to leave my work in the corporate sector, I wanted a fulfilling job. In order to meet the want, I had to understand what I needed. I knew that I wanted to continue helping people, and the path that I chose was to become a therapist. In order to become a therapist, I needed training and education, and in the state in which I reside (California), that also meant a master's degree. I *needed* my master's degree in order to fulfill my *want* of becoming a therapist.

Once I had completed the need, I had the allowance to safely pursue the want. I find therapy a limitless profession. I could go into teaching, presenting workshops, writing papers, supervising trainees and interns, and of course working with individuals, couples, and families. None of this would be possible if the need hadn't been met. Once that need had been met, I felt safe and secure to pursue a want—in my case a PhD. I didn't need a PhD to be a therapist, but I wanted a PhD to challenge myself and to deepen my understanding of human sexuality. Because the need had been met (obtaining my master's), even if I was unsuccessful in my pursuit of a PhD, it would have been okay because I had the base need met. I always had a safe place to return to.

When it comes to applying needs versus wants to an emotional experience such as love, I always start by asking clients what they need. What do you need in a partner(s)? What do you need to fulfill your sexuality? I often hear answers such as safety, patience, trust. And I also hear answers such as in shape, financially successful, or of a particular type. Do you need your partner to be in shape in order to feel safe in your relationship? If you can answer "No, I don't need my partner to be in shape, but it would be nice," that is a want and not a need. If you already feel safe with your partner, your need for safety has been met and you are then safe to explore other options that you may want in your life or relationship because you have a safe place to return to.

Ask yourself what do I need? If your needs are met, you have freedom to explore the wants. If your needs are not met, that is where the therapeutic work begins. How are your needs not being met? Are you aware of how they are not being met? What are the challenges that keep your needs from manifesting? Give yourself permission to explore your needs and your wants. Step into yourself and feel the shift that is possible. It may be the very thing you need in your life.

SOMACULTURAL LIBERATION: PUTTING IT ALL TOGETHER

By now you have completed your BOLD ADDRESSING assessment, reflected on your Triple Ps, examined your WOT, and gone through a four-spaces experiential. Hopefully you have begun to make connections about how the culture you were raised in and with shapes and informs your bodily experiences. I find all of this valuable, life-affirming, and life-changing information. So, what do we do with it? Simply knowing this information may be enough for many people. It may grant them some aha moments into why they feel the way they feel about certain people, experiences, and circumstances. If this is you, wonderful, but I still encourage you to take it a few steps further by applying a somacultural framework to as much of your lived experience as you can. Keeping a somacultural framework in your proverbial toolbox may help you with ongoing and new challenges you experience. I suggest utilizing two additional tools: goals and values, and what I call Soma-C.

Since becoming a licensed psychotherapist and certified sex therapist, I have been utilizing goals and values in the work I engage in with clients. I also use goals and values in my life. I find that setting clear goals and then using a particular set of values to help achieve those goals makes the process less complicated and within greater reach. I believe that at any given moment in our lives, we are operating within a particular set of values. These values may be personal, familial, or cultural. An example of a personal value is organization—keeping one's home and work organized. An example of family values is connection—celebrating holidays and birthdays together. An example of cultural values is compliance—honoring laws that ensure safety of others (such as traffic laws). Sometimes we operate within value systems without acknowledging we are doing so; we just do it. How did we learn about these values and are they truly our values, or are they values we have been told we must comply with? Using a somacultural liberatory framework means the values we are utilizing are of our choosing and do not intentionally inflict harm upon others.

How do we know what our values are and what values work best for the goals we hope to accomplish? I use a technique called the *fab five*. I choose five values from my values toolbox (more about that in a moment) to help me move closer to my goals. There is no particular magic behind the fab five. Rather, I choose (and recommend the same to you) five values to work with at any given time because I can easily remember the ones I have chosen using the digits of my dominant hand (in my case, my right hand) as a reference point.

Starting with my hand open, each time I name one of my fab five I bring a finger down to meet my palm. When I have named all five, my hand has naturally formed a fist and I then thrust my fist into the air and proclaim my power. It has been an empowering daily somatic practice I engage with. Since I have been practicing my fab-five technique, I am more focused, more energized, more grounded, and less anxious. I have also found I am able to accomplish my goals at a more even pace that suits my overall nervous system better.

An important thing to remember is values are fluid. We can change our fab five on a daily, weekly, monthly, or yearly basis—user's choice! Although I generally have the same set of values in my fab five, from time to time, I change them up as needed. While I was pursing my doctoral studies, the value of education was in my top five. The day I passed my dissertation defense and my dissertation committee said, "Congratulations, Dr. Kuhn!" I no longer needed to prioritize the value of education. It was an incredible relief to gently return the value of education to my toolbox and know it is there should I ever need to use it again. As I have been writing this book, my fab five have included the values of courage, creativity, discipline, vulnerability, and wellness. Each of these values has its own meaning to me and represents varying aspects of my overall book-writing process. Since I wrote *Somacultural Liberation* over the course of a year, I swapped out a fab-five value here and there as needed. For example, when I was not in book-writing mode, I did not need to prioritize the value of discipline. Instead, I would swap out the value of discipline and replace it with the value of connection, love, or pleasure, as examples. Once I was ready to start writing again, I would once again place discipline in my fab five. The values we choose to place in our fab five do not need to be values that we adore. I do not like being disciplined. I prefer to be more fluid in my day-to-day life, using my time outside of work in a freer-flowing fashion. That go-with-the-flow attitude unfortunately does not work for me from a writing perspective. If I am not disciplined and writing first thing in the morning (Hello, 5 a.m.!), I know myself enough to recognize that the likelihood of me writing at all that day is next to zero. Though, when I do prioritize the value of discipline, I get a lot of work done. Once this book is out of my hands, I guarantee you the value of discipline will be retired until I need to use it again.

I use the fab-five values with all my therapy clients, regardless of what they are coming to therapy for. I use the fab five as the first growth-work (aka homework) exercise I have clients do. I invite them to share their fab five with me during our next session. I make sure to make note of their fab five and strive to keep these in mind as we go through our work together. Whenever a client is feeling stuck or challenged with their goals, I ask them what value or values they believe are being impacted. If a client is unsure, because I have taken note of their fab five and what each of the values means to the client, I may be able to say, "It sounds like the value of 'connection' is being impacted here." I have found this to be an incredibly useful intervention to use with clients. It helps me better understand my clients, and I am told that when I reflect their values back to them, they feel seen and understood. It is also possible the value being impacted may not be in their fab five, though it is in their toolbox. When this is true, we spend time reflecting on the value being impacted and discuss what it would be like to prioritize that value in their fab five until the issue is resolved.

The following pages contain a list of values. I have purposely not provided the definitions for these values, as the point of this exercise is to understand what these values mean to you on a personal basis. Feel free to look the words up if you are not sure what they mean to assert your own interpretation. This values list is incomplete. If you hold a value that is not listed, please feel free to add that value to your toolbox. Your values toolbox contains the values you carry around with you on a day-to-day basis—the values that are always with you. It is from your values toolbox that you find your fab five and swap them out as needed.

Experiential: Fab-Five Values

Take a moment to review the following list of values. Go through each of the values and every time a value resonates with you, mark it with the letter T for "toolbox." Once you have gone through the list, go back and look at all the values you placed a T next to. Spend some time reflecting on what each means to you.

Next, think about a goal you are working toward in your life at the moment. This could be an immediate goal, such as doing a particular task within the next few days, or a broader goal, such as welcoming a romantic relationship into your life. Go through your toolbox values once again and choose the fab five you believe will bring you closer to achieving the current goal. If you have access to the digits on your hand, bring somatic awareness to these values by assigning each value to a digit; then name each value as you bring your fingers into a fist. You now have your fab-five power. They are there for you whenever you need them.

I also suggest writing these values down and putting them on your fridge, your mirror, your phone, or wherever you believe you will see them on a regular basis. If it feels right, share your fab five with a partner, family member, friend, or therapist. This list of values can also be found on my website, somaculturalliberation.com.

VALUES

acceptance
achievement
adventure
appreciation
approachability
artfulness
assertiveness
assurance
attractiveness
authenticity
authority
availability
autonomy
balance
beauty
boldness
caring
challenge
cleanliness
compassion
commitment
community
competency
consciousness
connection
confidence
conformity
containment
contribution
control
cooperation
courage
creativity
curiosity
dignity
diligence
directness

discipline
discovery
dreaming
drive
duty
education
efficiency
embodiment
encouragement
equality
eroticism
excitement
fairness
fame
family of origin
family of creation
flexibility
flow
fluidity
focus
frankness
freedom
friendliness
frugality
forgiveness
fun
generosity
grace
gratitude
growth
happiness
harmony
health
honesty
honor
hospitality
humor

humility
imagination
impact
industry
independence
intelligence
intimacy
intuition
joy
justice
kindness
knowledge
leadership
learning
liberation
logic
love
loyalty
lust
mastery
mindfulness
modesty
moderation
monogamy
optimism
order
originality
open-mindedness
patience
peace
perfection
persistence
pleasure
popularity
power
practicality
pragmatism

preparedness
professionalism
prosperity
purity
reciprocity
recognition
recreation
relaxation
resilience
respect
responsibility
restraint
romance
safety
security
self-awareness
self-care
self-control
sensuality
service
sexuality
solitude
spirituality
skillfulness
stability
social justice
solidarity
status
success
supportiveness
sympathy
synergy
thoroughness
tranquility
transcendence
trust
truth
understanding
uniqueness
unity
usefulness
valor
variety
virtue
vision
vitality
vivacity
vulnerability
warmth
wealth
wellness
willingness
wisdom
wonder
worth
zeal
zest

SOMA-C

I believe when we learn to listen and feel into our bodies, we can utilize the power of choice. As previously mentioned, several modalities may be helpful in learning to listen and feel into your body. A method that I have developed is called *Soma-C*, which is an acronym I use when I feel in a state of dysregulation. Soma-C stands for:

Scan: Close your eyes and scan your body for sensations you are experiencing.

Observe: Notice any thoughts, feelings, stories, or emotions that may be present with the sensations.

Mindful Movement: Bring some kind of mindful movement in your body. This could be a deep breath, shaking your body, dancing, fluttering your lips, and so on.

Assess: Notice what, if anything, has shifted. If you do not feel that anything has shifted in your awareness, scan, observe, and utilize mindful movement once again.

Choice: Make a choice that best aligns with your values and goals.

Engaging in a Soma-C practice can be incredibly powerful. It encourages us to slow down and regulate our nervous system. Making choices with a dysregulated nervous system can lead to feelings of disappointment and regret.

Experiential: Soma-C

You can carry out this experiential in a couple of ways. You can complete the experiential in the moment with whatever may be present for you at this time. You can perform this experiential by taking a few moments to reflect on an area, a tension, or a conflict in your life (a rupture in a relationship, a work issue, a historical event, etc.). You can also do this experiential by watching or reading a news story that may be evocative for you. This experiential is appropriate as an intervention to use in a somatic practice, which might include psychotherapy or coaching.

To begin, find yourself in a comfortable and supportive position. Once you have settled, take a deep breath. Begin to scan your body noticing any areas of tension, any temperatures you may feel on your skin or in your internal system, any sensations that may be coursing through your body or at a localized spot on your body. Take a deep breath. Observe any thoughts, feelings, emotions, or stories that may be present. Take a deep breath. Begin to bring mindful movement to your body (this could be taking another deep breath, rocking back and forth or side to side, shaking your body, etc.). Take a deep breath. Assess how the body feels in this moment. What, if anything, may have shifted? Take a deep breath. Take a few moments to reflect on your experience and make a choice about how you would like to proceed. Spend 10 to 15 minutes writing about your experience and what you may have learned by engaging in the experiential.

NEXT STEPS

You are likely asking yourself, "Now what?" You've done your BOLD ADDRESSING model, you've incorporated Soma-C into your mindfulness practice, you've considered how who you are impacts what you know, and you've done some work around values. Now what? My answer: What do you want to do? You could hold this information dear to your heart and continue to process with yourself and with others. You could also share what you have learned about yourself and your culture with others. These are great examples, and since liberation is a subjective experience, you get to be the one who decides what it means to you. That is the power of choice and I hope you recognize you have it.

For me, it wasn't enough to understand my positionality and epistemology. I needed to do something with the information I had acquired. Yes, writing a book is an example of doing something, yet it wasn't enough for me. Although writing and sharing this information with all of you has been a liberating process, I never intended to be or deeply desired to be an author. Here's a bit of information that may surprise some of you: I do not enjoy this kind of writing. I knew that I could write a book because I had written a dissertation. For those of you unfamiliar with a dissertation, think of it as a really arduous research paper that requires you to follow strict guidelines around citations, grammar, and adherence to protocols to keep research participants safe. I found the process painful, and in the final month of my writing process, I cried on a daily basis. Now, in the final month of writing this book, I too am asking myself, "Now what?"

When I first conceptualized somacultural liberation, I was a PhD student full of wonder and curiosity. I was also healing the shame that surrounded my lack of education. When I completed the ultimate degree one can receive in higher education, I still did not feel liberated. Opportunities were coming my way for teaching jobs and keynote speaking gigs. My clinical practice was full, and I had a waiting list of clients wanting to work with me. I was making more money than I had ever made in my life. Truth be told, I was living happily unfulfilled.

I recently attended a gathering for Two-Spirit people hosted by the Montana Two Spirit Society. I made a bunch of new friends and had an amazing time. A few people I met already knew who I was; they said they had read some of my work or knew that I was an activist and an organizer of the BAAITS Powwow. None of them knew me for my true passion in life—music.

The gathering holds a talent-sharing evening where attendees share song, dance, poetry, stories, and drag performances. Anyone can sign up and even though I do have a performing background, I made the choice to not sign up to perform. I felt shy about sharing with this group of people who I felt incredibly comfortable around. At the show, there was a performer who sang a cover of one of my favorite songs, "Dancing on My Own," by the artist Robyn. Their performance was full of emotion, and they shared so freely. I was feeling envious while watching their performance. I wasn't envious of their singing ability; I was envious of the way they shared, with what I projected onto them as ease. I was envious of the applause they received for sharing their joy and passion.

The next morning, I woke up before sunrise and sat down by the lake to watch the sunrise. I replayed the previous evening in my mind and went into comparison mode. Despite the amazing year I had had, including being featured in an international campaign for Levi's, I couldn't shake the feeling that the performer was more accomplished than I was. My reasoning—they allowed themself to be seen.

You may think I do the same thing—allow myself to be seen—and you'd be correct. The difference is I only allow myself to be seen as accomplished. It is easy for me to show up as Dr. Roger Kuhn because the Dr. in front of my name signifies an accomplishment that I have made, whereas music has long been elusive and an area in my life in which I do not feel accomplished enough, making it very challenging for me to share what is my true passion. Nothing gives me the feeling of liberation in my body that singing does. It doesn't matter if I am singing a song I wrote or singing a song someone else wrote. I can sing about joy, pain, desire, or grief, and I still feel liberated.

As the sun rose that morning, I found myself crying once again. I called myself a fraud and asked myself how I could profess an ideology of somacultural liberation while not doing the thing that makes me feel most liberated. I called my husband, Sean, and shared my feelings with him. He listened attentively and when I was finished, he simply asked, "What do you want to do about it?" I paused for a moment, did a quick Soma-C practice, and answered, "I'm going to sing again."

In 2008, I made the choice to no longer pursue music as a viable career. I chose to only perform every few years and no longer promoted any of the music I had created. I told myself it was because I had found the true love I was looking for and therefore the love I felt while performing was moot. I didn't allow myself to have both. I looked at my music career as a failure because I didn't make it as a rock star. I did not recognize I had the choice in how I defined my own success.

If you seek out my music, you will easily find it on all streaming platforms. I even have a music video you can watch on YouTube. The video is for a song I wrote called "What's Your Name." The video played on national television and the Logo TV named the video one of the top ten videos of 2008. When my video first debuted on the Logo channel's *The Click List*, I came in at number 9. The number 10 spot was held by my rock icon, Melissa Etheridge. The song, "What's Your Name," was also awarded Song of the Year by The Stonewall Society for the Arts. I have recorded and released four albums of original music, including an album of holiday-themed music. My music has been played on radio stations in the US and Canada and I was also featured in a nationally distributed LGBTQ+ magazine. Yet, because I couldn't live off of the money I made as a musician, I considered my art and music a failure.

When I ended the call with Sean, I made the choice to no longer see myself as a failure. I realized the only time I can fail is if I do nothing about my music to begin with. I was not a failure; I had accomplished a lot with my music and could always accomplish more. My key to liberation as a musician is to be seen for who I am.

By the time this book is in your hands, I will have released my fifth album, this one a compilation of the favorite songs I have ever written and four new original songs. The album, available on vinyl or streaming, is titled *Mvto*, the Muscogee word for thank you. *Mvto* is a thank you letter to my family, friends, and music fans who have supported me over the years. It is also a thank you letter to myself for embracing who I am. I am a rock star who also happens to be an activist, artist, writer, husband, son, brother, best friend, therapist, educator, and video game lover. I am on a path toward liberation, and I help others on their path as well. You have the tools to embrace who you are. I encourage you to pursue what is in your heart, as that is where our true liberation lives.

Experiential: Connecting to Your Passion

Set aside 10 to 15 minutes for this experiential. Find a journal or something you can take notes on such as a phone, computer, or tablet. Take a deep breath. What is a passion of yours that you no longer pursue or have never pursued? What is the story you have associated with not following through with this passion? Take a deep breath. Take 5 minutes to write the story of not following through with your passion. Take a deep breath. Do a Soma-C practice. What choice will you make about following through with your passion? Take another 10 to 15 minutes to write about how you plan to do this. Give yourself a one-day, one-week, one-month, and six-month goal around following through on your passion. Use your values to help you get there.

SOMACULTURAL CASE STUDY

For any therapists/clinicians reading this book, you may wonder how a somacultural liberatory framework is helpful in a session or as a clinical intervention. If you are not a clinician, but do participate in therapy or self-growth work (what some call self-help), this section may help you understand how clinicians conceptualize interventions that are utilized in sessions and as out-of-session growth-work experientials.

As I mentioned at the beginning of this book, I work as a psychotherapist in private practice with a specialty in sex therapy. The following case study exemplifies how utilizing a somacultural framework aids the client and the therapist/educator with understanding the nuanced intersection of social media, online sexual imagery, out-of-control sexual behavior, erectile challenges, and sexual identity.

CASE BACKGROUND

With access to social media sites such as Meta and search engines such as Google, the ubiquitous phrase "everyone is an expert" is increasingly becoming more of a reality. Although the Internet can help with a variety of tips, tricks, and techniques, it can also be a bastion of oppressive content (Noble, 2018) and false or misinformed diagnostic information when it comes to medical or psychological symptoms that a person may be experiencing. Technology, including the Internet and Wi-Fi, is also not globally accessible. Many rural communities, including reservation communities in North America, continue to lack infrastructure to make access to the Internet and Wi-Fi possible.

Social media and online search engines increase user accessibility to content that may complement their sexuality by offering a forum in which to meet others with similar or the same gender presentation, sexual orientation, and sexual behaviors. Yet, despite the advances and access social media and online search engines have enabled for individuals, groups, or entities, for some, sexuality remains a deeply private matter, one they may feel uncomfortable exploring in their lives.

This is where a somacultural framework can support clients who are working with a sexual issue that may be impacting their life. This issue could be physiological such as erectile dysfunction in penis-bodied individuals or genitopelvic pain disorder in vulva-bodied individuals. The issue could also be related to intimacy issues including body image or out-of-control sexual behavior (OCSB). Additionally, it is important to consider the sociocultural and somatic aspects that may be playing a role in the phenomena the client is experiencing.

In the case of Nyle,* a self-diagnosis of sex and porn addiction, including Internet sexual imagery usage, led the twenty-six-year-old mixed-race (Asian and Black) gay cisgender male to seek therapy. Nyle also suffered from what he described as porn-induced erectile dysfunction. Throughout the course of our year-long therapeutic relationship, cultural themes such as masculinity, OCSB, online sexual imagery, sexual performance anxiety, daddy/boy relationships, and sexual desire have been investigated to support a deepening of his epistemological understanding of self.

* Client name and defining characteristics have been changed to protect confidentiality.

Nyle is the only child of a first-generation Chinese mother, who was his primary caregiver, and a Black father from the American South. Nyle was born and raised in San Francisco, where he currently lives and works as a software engineer for a large tech conglomerate. He is above-average height, has the somatotype of a mesomorph, and self-defines as a muscle cub with a kink for pup play.[†] He does not have any religious affiliation, though he self-identifies as spiritual. He has been experiencing erectile challenges and intermittent anodyspareunia since his early twenties. At the beginning of his therapy, he attended weekly Sex Addicts Anonymous (SAA) meetings and had a sponsor with whom he spoke daily. He did not own a personal computer out of fear that his desire for sexual imagery, including pornography, would be too strong. Additionally, he had blocks on his phone that restricted access to adult content.

The treatment goals that were established at the beginning of the work included reducing porn consumption, reducing anxiety around sexual performance issues including erectile challenges, reducing body image issues, and processing shame. One of the first cultural interventions that was offered in our work was reframing sexual addiction to OCSB (Braun-Harvey & Vigorito, 2016). I use the term *cultural intervention* to highlight the differing ideologies behind using a sexual addiction framework and an OCSB framework. I use an OCSB framework in my clinical practice and worked with Doug Braun-Harvey as my primary supervisor when completing my Sex Therapist certification through the American Association of Sexuality Educators, Counselors and Therapists (AASECT).

Out-of-Control Sexual Behavior

The *Diagnostic and Statistical Manuel of Mental Disorders*, 5th Edition (DSM-5) (APA, 2013) describe sexual dysfunctions as "a heterogeneous group of disorders that are typically characterized by a clinically significant disturbance in a person's ability to respond sexually or to experience

---

† A *muscle cub* is defined as a gay male between the ages of eighteen and thirty-five with an above-average build and frame with muscular definition. *Pup play* is a form of autozoophilia wherein participants engage in activities, manners, and behaviors akin to canines.

sexual pleasure" (p. 423). Sexual dysfunctions include, but are not limited to, erectile disorder (302.72) and other specified sexual dysfunction (302.79). Currently, the DSM-5 does not have a diagnostic consideration for sexual addiction, sexual compulsion, or out-of-control sexual behavior. Braun-Harvey and Vigorito (2016) define OCSB as "a sexual problem of consensual sexual urges, thoughts, or behaviors that feel out of control for the individual" (p. 310). There is no agreed-upon standard of what constitutes an addiction, which makes obtaining evidence of a sexual addiction challenging and assertions without similar studies within human sexual behavior are "speculative and unsupported" (p. 4). They add a cautionary note that the addiction model may limit our understanding by offering an overly simplistic view of the diverse issues encountered by this clinical population. OCSB is a counterpoint to the terms *sex addict* or *sexual addiction*. Sex addict and sexual addiction first found prominence in the late 1970s/early 1980s and gained widespread notoriety in the public throughout the decades that followed (Reay, Attwood, & Gooder, 2012). The roots of sex addiction come from addiction models involving alcohol and chemical dependence. One of the most popular models of sex addiction recovery is Sex Addicts Anonymous (SAA), modeled after Alcoholics Anonymous (AA). Like AA, SAA is a twelve-step model to help participants heal and make amends for past behaviors. SAA meetings happen daily around the world.

One of the complications in our work has been Nyle's access to stimulating material. The sexual imagery consumption that Nyle struggles with is very easy to access. It has been just over three decades since the first smartphone, defined as a mobile device that incorporates both telecommunications and personal computing, was made available for mass audiences. Since the release of the Simon Personal Communicator in 1994, smartphone technology has transitioned from a device that could receive emails to devices that can stream content, including sexual imagery, in any location where the user has access to a Wi-Fi signal. Recent advances in mobile technology have also seen the creation and distribution of apps that use geolocation services on personal smart devices to locate potential sex partners.

Queer theorists (Brown, Maycock, & Burns, 2005; Mowlabocus, 2010; Ross, 2005) have explored how technology manifests in the lives of the

2SLGBTQIA+ community. As technology evolved, global position systems (GPS) and geolocation positioning (GLP) were added to smartphones and helped pave the way for mobile apps such as Grindr (2009), Scruff (2010), and Jack'd (2012), which provide users with an opportunity to locate others who are also using the apps for conversation, dates, friendship, or sex. Brown et al. (2005) recognize the Internet as a place where gay men can go without the fear of negative social consequences. Ross (2005) argues "the internet, while not transforming sexuality, has transfigured it: it has illuminated certain aspects of it so that they stand out from their equivalent social sexual interactions" (p. 342). Mowlabocus (2010) highlights the importance of understanding that gay social networking apps (GSNA) "depend on users moving through physical space and this dependence creates complex and a myriad of relationships with different types of space" (p. 187). Prior to the mobile revolution, people were confined to private or public spaces where one could access the Internet over a stationary computer or laptop. Any interactions people may have had were limited to dial-up modems, privacy, and time dedicated to being online. New technology enables users to access GSNA from all over the world, at home, at the beach, or on the go. Potentially partners are now mere feet away. For Nyle, and clients struggling with OCSB, these apps can have deleterious impacts on social functioning and sexual excitation.

Nyle stopped going to meetings approximately two months into our work. The following cultural themes have been examined over the course of our three-year therapeutic alliance: race, age, sexual behavior, LGBTQ+ identity, power exchange, technology, and physiological issues relating to sexual performance. The following exchange, and those that follow, reflect paraphrased interactions that took place during our sessions.

N: I feel guilty that I no longer attend meetings.

R: Tell me about it.

N: It's like I'm afraid they are going to judge me.

R: Who is they, Nyle?

He laughs at the question and explains he was referring to the members of the SAA support group he attended on Tuesday evenings.

N: They are supposed to be my friends. I went to a potluck last weekend and everyone was worried about me. They are afraid that I'm going to slip, that I'm somehow fucking with my sobriety.

Unlike sobriety in AA, sobriety in SAA is not necessarily adhered to as an abstinence-only model (SAA, 2016). Rather, participants in SAA self-define their sobriety, which can include abstinence or sexual contact that could be limited to one partner. For Nyle, sobriety includes abstinence from masturbation induced through pornographic content and sex with one partner.

I sense something important about the impact of community that Nyle is mentioning, and I want to be sure we both understand the cultural implication that community plays in his life.

R: Tell me about any importance you place on the role of community in your life.

N: I never had community growing up. It's one of the reasons why I turned to my computer and video games. I have more of an online community. Online community is where I learned about sex and what I like. It's also where I learned that I was a sex addict and where I discovered local SAA meetings.

Nyle shares that he is active in several online communities including FetLife and Second Life, social networking sites Facebook and Instagram, and applications Grindr and Scruff.

R: Nyle, I'm wondering if you can share how you determined you were a sex addict?

N: I've been using pornography since I was thirteen years old. I think I searched gay on Google, and it eventually led me to a porn site and as they say, the rest is history.

R: Do you remember what your earlier experiences with sexual imagery were?

N: I remember never seeing guys that looked like me. Mostly I saw White guys, sometimes Latin and Black guys. If I did see Asian guys, they were always small and always bottoming.

In this exchange, Nyle is referencing how algorithms influenced the sexual imagery content he is encountering. We further explore what it is like for him to not see himself represented.

> *N: Because I was raised by my mom in an Asian household I've always identified more as Asian. I grew up thinking that I had to be a bottom because I was Asian. I exclusively bottomed for the first eight years of being sexually active (he shares he had his first sexual experience at seventeen and has never had sex with someone who identified as female). When I did try to top for the first time, I lost my erection after a few minutes and to be honest, I don't think I've ever been able to successfully top.*

Nyle appears to grow uncomfortable with the topic. I pause our conversation and bring his focus to the present moment.

> *R: Can you tell me what you are feeling right now, Nyle?*
>
> *N: Shame. Guilt. Sadness.*
>
> *R: Can you tell me how shame feels?*
>
> *N: What do you mean?*
>
> *R: I wonder if you can name any sensations you feel in your body when you feel shame.*
>
> *N: In my chest, I feel it in my chest. It's a tight feeling. Like a tight ball of wires, full of electricity, ready to pop out of my body at any moment.*

The concept of shame has been a theme throughout our work. When Nyle and I first began working with each other, shame and guilt were often processed. According to Sedgwick (2008), "the conventional way of distinguishing shame from guilt is that shame attaches to and sharpens the sense of what one is, whereas guilt attaches to what one does" (p. 51). Using Sedgwick's model, we could quantify Nyle's shame from a somacultural perspective as being partly rooted in his mixed-race identity, his sexual orientation, and his usage of sexual imagery. Shame continues to perpetuate in gay male culture, which for some men continues to have injurious implications to their sexual health and wellness. The feeling of shame is something that many gay men understand and can be additionally troubling for gay men with sexual compulsion (Braun-Harvey & Vigorito, 2016). The shaming leads to a vicious cycle wherein "the expression of sexual feelings, having previously been met with shame and/or ridicule give rise to overwhelming feelings of shame; sexual activity provides comfort for this discomforting affect, which in turn elicits further shame that is relieved by more sex" (Gosling, 2000, p. 144). A pattern of repetition is then produced, which leads to compulsion (Braun-Harvey & Vigorito, 2016).

Daddy's Boy

In the sessions that follow, Nyle shares that he has had over fifty sexual partners over the course of his life. Of those fifty, he has experienced receptive anal penetration with all of them and has attempted assertive anal penetration with fewer than five. According to the literature on the topic of sex roles in gay culture, "top, bottom, or versatile self-labeling may not merely indicate role preference during anal intercourse [and] research suggests that individuals may find it reflective of other aspects such as gender typicality and sexual power" (Moskowitz, Rieger, & Roloff, 2008, p. 192). Additionally, "there is evidence to suggest that men who have sex with men (MSM) may also associate these terms with gender roles" (Johns, Pingel, Eisenberg, Santana, & Bauermeister, 2012, p. 3). Nyle speaks of the perceived gender identity of bottoms, stating his displeasure for being seen as femme. He prides himself on being a muscle cub and revels in the perceived social status that gives him among his peers, including a former sexual partner, Jacob, a White cisgender gay male fifteen years his senior whom he had a daddy/boy relationship with.

When exploring the phenomena of "daddy and boy (or boi)" in gay relationships, in some cases it may be possible that "cross-generational desire is explored through the lens of physical and emotional desire for our fathers" (Lugar, 2013, p. 153). In the case of Nyle, we explore the cultural significance of an absent father as well as his desire for older sexual partners and his belief that he must be in a submissive sexual role due to his Asian identity. Daddy and boy plays into the narrative of submission—asking for permission, obeying orders, showing respect, using proper manners, and so on. When Nyle first shared about his daddy and boy relationship, I believed it was important that we explore the somacultural aspects of what this relationship meant to him.

N: Sometimes I feel that Jacob is the only person that understands how I feel. He doesn't judge my experience. Even if I can't get hard, he says it's okay. It's okay if we just cuddle.

R: What part of yourself do you get to experience through his support?

N: I get to feel love. What you refer to as my light side. Am I saying that right, light versus shadow? Yes, my light side. I get to experience my light side.

Nyle states he wants to bottom for Jacob because he wants to give him pleasure. I ask him what is behind his desire to give Jacob pleasure and he answers, "*closeness.*" I offer the word intimacy. He pauses, takes a deep breath, and says, "Yes, I want intimacy with Jacob." I ask if there are other ways he can achieve intimacy with Jacob and he replies that he has intimacy with him already in many ways, but bottoming for Jacob, giving Daddy pleasure in this way, is what he desires most.

R: Who is the intimacy for?

N: The surrender is for him; the pleasure is for both of us. I get pleasure when I see him experience pleasure.

R: How about the pain? Do you experience any of the anal pain when being a receptive partner?

Nyle looks out the window and sighs. He sticks his tongue out and slightly bites down, a somatic cue that I have come to know means he is experiencing a heightened state of excitation.

R: Reminder that you do not have to answer any of the questions that I ask.

N: Of course, I do. Not always, not all the time. Poppers help.

He laughs at this point and gives me a smile and a nod.

Over several sessions, we also begin to explore how age and race have been addressed in the relationship, with Nyle sharing that Jacob won't let him top because he is too young, and Jacob wants him to be submissive.

Nyle reacts to Jacob's request of submission as Jacob's entitlement to his body because of their racial differences.

> *N: He doesn't explicitly call me any racist names, though he has laughed at jokes his friends have made about Asian and Black people.*

> *R: What happens to your body when you witness that?*

> *N: I feel small. I don't want to have sex with him. I want to pull away, hide. I contract.*

Contraction is a state that Nyle is familiar with and has shared that he has been contracting for as long as he could remember. He has contracted when people made fun of his sexuality, racial identity, hair texture and body size, and when sexual partners have exotified him.

To work with his contracted state, we have engaged in various somatic exercises including breathwork to feel his rib and lungs expand, full-body tense and relax exercises to feel how holding his body in a hypervigilant posture impacts his capacity to expand, and a hand-based exercise that explores his present relationship with his sexual behavior and what he imagines is possible if he is able to make the changes in his life he is seeking. Additionally, we have utilized guided visualization, pelvic bowl relaxation, and breathwork to work with his erectile challenges and anodyspareunia.

Therapeutic Alliance as a Somacultural Intervention

The therapeutic alliance that happens through a somacultural framework can be viewed as "most essential to the change process" (Braun-Harvey & Vigorito, 2016, p. 261) because it is through this framework that clients understand that their experiences are valid and will be met with compassion, nonjudgment, and unconditional positive regard. Stolorow, Brandchaft, and Atwood (1987) propose "the only reality relevant and accessible to psychoanalytic inquiry is subjective reality—that of the patient, that of the analyst, and the psychological field created by the interplay between the two" (p. 4). This subjective reality is based upon the lived experiences and subjective worlds of the client and the therapist and "is always empathic or introspective" (Stolorow et al., 1987,

p. 5). Braun-Harvey and Vigorito (2016) ask, "How do your life experiences and sexual values influence your work? How do you resolve personal and professional discomfort with detailed sexual health conversations?" (p. 303). My identity as a mixed-race Poarch Creek Two-Spirit Indigiqueer sexually fluid male is present in the therapeutic work. Nyle has often shared that my identity is one of the reasons he feels so comfortable in our work together. As Nyle is walking to our weekly appointments, he does so under the shadow of the gay flag, which he has commented gives him a sense of belonging, identity, and community.

Nyle has inquired about my Internet usage and holds curiosity about whether I am in a relationship or not. According to Prenn (2009), self-disclosure "is neither good nor bad; it is the quickest way to have an experience between two people" (p. 89). I use self-disclosure to facilitate dialogue between Nyle and myself to resolve his curiosity so that we can continue with the work.

N: Are you in a relationship?

R: Yes, I am.

N: How long?

R: It's been fifteen years now.

N: Wow, that must be nice to not feel lonely. Are you married?

R: I am. I have worn my wedding ring to every session.

N: Are you and your husband open?

R: No, we are monogamous. Tell me, Nyle, what is it like to know this about me?

N: It humanizes you. It helps me have hope. That maybe someday I too can find love. Does your husband know about me?

R: He knows that I have clients, but he doesn't know any details about my clients.

N: So, you don't talk about me?

R: I think about you when we are not in session, and we agreed to a confidential relationship. I honor that.

N: That's good. I appreciate that. Do you have a good sex life?

He laughs as he asks this question.

Nyle's question about my personal sex life did not strike me as odd. I find it natural that a client may have a curiosity about my sex life, considering I am clear with clients that one of my areas of focus is sexual health and wellness. Though this case study does not cover transference or erotic transference, it is imperative that clinicians working in the field of sex therapy and using a somacultural framework be mindful that erotic transference may be present in sessions. If so, the clinician should seek consultation should the transference become a challenge.

Nyle continues weekly therapy sessions, and we have worked together for almost three years, including online during the Covid-19 pandemic. He continues to make considerable improvements in the anxiety he feels around sexuality and no longer refers to himself as a sex addict. He ended his relationship with Jacob and has reevaluated his relationship to sexual imagery. Using mindfulness techniques such as breathing, body tracking, and tense and release exercises that have been introduced and practiced since the beginning of our work, Nyle reports that when he feels an urge to use pornography to numb his pain, he can use these techniques to remain present and ride the wave of anxiety until he feels the electric feeling in his chest subside.

Nyle self-selected to stop using the term sex addict after reframing his past behavior through a new understanding of the way culture influenced some of his sexual choices. He has removed all the parental blocks from his phone and has purchased a home computer for both personal and work use. He continues to struggle with feelings of isolation and abandonment and continues to express a desire to be a part of community.

Applying a somacultural ideology to the work we have done together has enabled Nyle to examine the role culture has played in his bodily experiences. He reports a greater sense of being content with his relationship to his mixed-race identity, his sexuality, and his body. He is currently dating one member of a polyamorous couple who also identifies as Asian and Black. They have a versatile sexual relationship and Nyle reports infrequent anodyspareunia and has not experienced any erectile challenges since their first sexual experience together. When I ask him how it feels to not be experiencing anal pain or erectile challenges, he smiles and says, “liberating.”

CONCLUSION: RETURNING TO OURSELVES

Since I began to conceptualize the theory and ideology of somacultural liberation, the culture in which I live has changed. Because my positionality is inherently impacted by the culture I live in, with, and experience, the fluidity of culture and the impact it has on my body is an ever-evolving phenomenon. Positions of power have changed hands the world over, loved ones have transitioned to the afterlife, and new thoughts, ideas, music, film, and books have influenced how I understand the world around me and how I feel and experience my body. The same is, no doubt, true for you as well. Also, because I wrote this book in various locations, I was impacted by the culture in the places I was writing. In my homeland territory of the Poarch Creek Nation, I was anticipating my writing to have a depth, richness, and ease; unfortunately that did not happen. Although I did get a lot of writing accomplished while I was on the reservation, it did not grant me the serenity I had anticipated. Most times when I am visiting the reservation, I am focused on my time with my mom, sisters, aunties, uncles, cousins, and tribal members whom I consider friends. While writing this book, I visited my reservation four times. Each time I was reminded of what the reservation stood for—genocide, lies, deceit, and resilience. I had to take many walks while I was writing on the reservation because I noticed my body tensing and anxiety coursing through my system. Although I love being on the reservation, especially being with my family, when I leave, it is a harsh reminder that I am now in the state of Alabama, where a body and a culture that I espouse are not always welcome. Alabama does not have any protections for 2SLGBTQIA+ people other than allowing and recognizing same-sex marriage, though only because of *Obergefell v. Hodges*, which legalized same-sex marriage in the United States in 2015. Though I may feel safer on the reservation, going to and leaving the reservation requires me to interact with a culture that I believe would rather I not exist in the first place. I often feel my body is in a state of constriction when I am in Alabama.

Yet, I know that many of you reading this book may not have the opportunity to be on the land of your ancestors as often as I am. Even when I am in "Alabama," I am in Muscogee territory. Just because the government stole our land and forced most of my maternal ancestors off does not make the land any less Muscogee. That is our land, that is our home. Over the years my relationship with the state of Alabama has evolved, and I feel less constricted and more liberated in my body. My edge says, "Fuck around and find out," though my heart says, "You belong here, Rog." I do belong in Muscogee territory, now known as Alabama. I will always belong in Alabama because Alabama is home. It is where my mom lives, where my sister and her husband live. It is where I have my aunties and uncles, hundreds of cousins, and a community of tribal members who love me, support me, and want me to succeed in this colonized world. It is the home of my ancestors.

In her book *Spiral to the Stars: Mvskoke Tools of Futurity* (2019), writer Laura Harjo states that wherever she goes, it becomes a Muscogee place. Harjo does not claim ownership of the land; rather she is suggesting her cultural understandings as a Muscogee person inform how she feels in her body when she is in different places and among cultures that may differ from her own. I concur with this idea and believe the same is true for all of us. Wherever we go, we see and understand place through our own positionality and epistemology. This does not mean we can lay any claim to ownership, nor does it give us any authority to appropriate culture. It simply means we will always see the world around us, the land around us, the people and culture around us from our own unique understanding. What we do with this understanding can bring us closer to liberation or tear us apart inside. I choose, and I hope you do as well, to always take the path that will bring me closer to liberation, even if I do not understand in the moment. I may never understand, and in those cases I may choose to remove myself from a particular environment that I find harmful to my body, mind, emotions, and spirit.

Somacultural liberation is one path of returning to ourselves. When you practice the techniques I have shared throughout this book, I hope you understand who you are and what you know in a new way. I hope this knowledge helps you unpack some of the complications you have had in your life that may have led your body, your system, to feel contraction. I hope you can feel a sense of expansion, what I also call liberation, in your body through learning about somacultural liberation. If you do, I hope you will share this knowledge with your family, your children, your friends, your community, and maybe even with a stranger.

The stories that I have shared throughout this book are just that, stories. Although they may be stories from my lived experiences, I recognize my stories do not necessarily make me who I am. How I feel about those stories is always where my work lies. I believe the same is true for you. How we feel about our bodies, our culture, our stories, is always where our work lies. We cannot change history, nor can we change what has happened to us, or for us. Because culture is an ever-shifting phenomena, our stories will also shift, which means our bodies will shift too.

To return to ourselves means to come home to our bodies. Coming home to our bodies means we find the liberation, the expansion, we need to pursue our goals, dreams, ambitions, and healing with as much strength, courage, and vulnerability as needed. Take a breath with me and know that returning to ourselves is a pleasurable experience, and pleasure heals.

REFERENCES

Alexie, S. (Director). (2002). *The Business of Fancydancing* [Motion picture on DVD]. USA: Falls Apart Productions.

Angelino, H., & Shedd, C. (1955). A note on Berdache. *American Anthropologist, 57*(1), 121–126.

APA. (2013). *Diagnostic and statistical manual of mental disorders: DSM-5.* Arlington, VA: American Psychiatric Publishing.

Audergon, A. (2004). Collective trauma: The nightmare of history. *Psychotherapy and Politics International,* 2(1), 16–31. https://doi.org/10.1002/ppi.67

Bakshi, S., Jivraj, S., & Posocco, S. (Eds.). (2016). *Decolonizing sexualities: Transnational perspectives, critical interventions.* Oxford, England: Counterpress.

Balsam, K. F., Huang, B., Fieland, K. C., Simoni, J. M., & Walters, K. L. (2004). Culture, trauma, and wellness: A comparison of heterosexual and gay, bisexual, and two-spirit Native Americans. *Cultural Diversity and Ethnic Minority Psychology, 10*(3), 287–301.

Bartlett, A., & Tran, N. (2019, July 1). SF Pride Parade 2019: The most colorful costumes and creative signs. *SFGATE.* https://www.sfgate.com/entertainment/article/Pride-2019-Clever-costumes-signs-san-francisco-14062549.php

Bezucha, T. (Director). (2000.). *Big Eden* [Motion picture]. USA: Chaiken Films.

Braun-Harvey, D., & Vigorito, M. A. (2016). *Treating out of control sexual behavior: Rethinking sex addiction.* New York, NY: Springer Publishing Company, LLC.

Brown, B. (2021). *Atlas of the heart.* New York, NY: Random House.

Brown, G., Maycock, B., & Burns, S. (2005). Your picture is your bait: Use and meaning of cyberspace among gay men. *Journal of Sex Research, 42*(1), 63–73. https://doi.org/10.1080/00224490509552258

Brown, L. B. (1997). *Two spirit people: American Indian, lesbian women and gay men.* New York, NY: Routledge.

Buchanan, P. J. (1987, December 2). AIDS and moral bankruptcy. *New York Post*, 23.

Buescher, D. T., & Ono, K. A. (1996). Civilized colonialism: Pocahontas as neocolonial rhetoric. *Women's Studies in Communication, 19*, 127–153.

Burns, R. (1988). Preface. In W. Roscoe (Ed.), *Living the spirit: A gay American Indian anthology*. New York, NY: St. Martin's Press.

Butler, J. (1990). *Gender trouble: Feminism and the subversion of identity*. New York, NY: Routledge.

Callender, C. & Kochems, L. M. (1983, Aug–Oct.). The North American berdache. *Current Anthropology, 24*(4), 443–470.

Callimachi, R. (2021, November 17). Lost lives, lost culture: The forgotten history of indigenous boarding schools. *New York Times.* Retrieved June 29, 2023 from https://www.nytimes.com/2021/07/19/us/us-canada-indigenous-boarding-residential-schools.html

Cameron, M. (2005). Two-Spirited Aboriginal people. *Canadian Women's Studies, 24*(2,3), 123–127.

Collins, P. H. (2005). *Black sexual politics: African Americans, gender, and the new racism.* New York, NY: Routledge.

Crenshaw, K. (1989). Demarginalizing the intersection of race and sex: A Black feminist critique of antidiscrimination doctrine, feminist theory and antiracist politics. *University of Chicago Legal Forum, 1989*(1), 139–167. https://chicagounbound.uchicago.edu/cgi/viewcontent.cgi?article=1052&context=uclf

Crenshaw, K. (1991). Mapping the margins: Intersectionality, identity politics, and violence against women of color. *Stanford Law Review, 43*(6), 1241–1299. https://doi.org/10.2307/1229039

Degruy, J. (2005). *Post traumatic slave syndrome: America's legacy of enduring injury and healing.* Portland, OR: Uptone Press.

Dillon, G. L. (Ed.). (2012). *Walking the clouds: An anthology of indigenous science fiction.* Tucson, AZ: University of Arizona Press.

DinéYazhi, D. (Ed.). (2015). *Survivance—Indigenous poesis* (Vol. 1). Portland, OR: Radical Indigenous Survivance & Empowerment.

Driskill, Q. (2011a). Asegi Ayetl: Cherokee two-spirit people reimagining nation. In Q. Driskill, C. Finley, B. Gilley, & S. Morgensen (Eds.), *Queer indigenous studies: Critical interventions in theory, politics, and literature* (pp. 97–112). Tucson, AZ: University of Arizona Press.

Driskill, Q. (2011b). In Q. Driskill, D. Justice, D. Miranda, & L. Tatonetti (Eds.), *Sovereign erotics: A collection of Two-Spirit literature* (pp. 86–88). Tucson, AZ: University of Arizona Press.

Epple, C. (1998). Coming to terms with Navajo "nádleehí": A critique of "berdache," "gay," "alternate gender," and "Two-Spirit." *American Ethnologist, 25*(2), 267–290.

Estrada, G. (2011). Two-Spirit histories in Southwestern and Mesoamerican literature. In S. Slater & F. Yarbrough (Eds.), *Gender and sexuality in Indigenous North America, 1400–1850* (pp. 165–184). Columbia, SC: University of South Carolina Press.

Finley, C. (2011). Decolonizing the Queer Native body (and recovering the Native bull-dyke): Bringing "sexy back" and out of Native Studies' closet. In Q. Driskill, C. Finley, B. Gilley, & S. Morgensen (Eds.), *Queer Indigenous studies: Critical interventions in theory, politics, and literature* (pp. 31–42). Tucson, AZ: University of Arizona Press.

Fisher, H. E. (2005). *Why we love: The nature and chemistry of romantic love.* New York, NY: Henry Holt.

Foucault, M. (1978). *The history of sexuality: Volume 1, an introduction* (R. Hurley, Trans.). New York, NY: Vintage.

Garrett, M., & Barret, B. (2003). Two Spirit: Counseling Native American gay, lesbian, and bisexual people. *Journal of Multicultural Counseling and Development 31*(2), 131–142.

Gilley, B. J. (2006). *Becoming Two-Spirit: Gay identity and social acceptance in Indian country.* Lincoln, NE: University of Nebraska Press.

Gilley, B. J. (2011). Two-Spirit men's sexual survivance against the inequality of desire. In Q. Driskill, C. Finley, B. Gilley, & S. Morgensen (Eds.), *Queer Indigenous studies: Critical interventions in theory, politics, and literature* (pp. 123–131). Tucson, AZ: University of Arizona Press.

Goodyear, S. (2021, June 25). As Canada grapples with Residential School Legacy, the U.S. looks to its own history. CBC Radio. https://www.cbc.ca/radio/asithappens/residential-schools-us-boarding-schools-investigation-remains-1.6078723

Gosling, J. A. (2000). Sexual compulsivity in gay men from a Jungian perspective. *Journal of Gay & Lesbian Psychotherapy, 3*(3–4), 141–167. https://doi.org/10.1300/j236v03n03_11

Goulet, J. (1996). The 'berdache'/'Two-Spirit': A comparison of anthropological and native constructions of gendered identities among the Northern Athapaskans. *The Journal of the Royal Anthropological Institute, 2*(4), 683–701.

Harjo, S. (2010). Just good sports: The impact of "Native" references in sports on Native youth and what some decolonizers have done about it. In W. A. Wilson & M. Yellow Bird (Eds.), *For indigenous eyes only: A decolonization handbook* (pp. 31–52). Santa Fe, NM: School of American Research.

Harjo, L. (2019). *Spiral to the stars. Mvskoke tools of Futurity.* Tucson, AZ: University of Arizona Press.

Hartmann, W. E., Wendt, D. C., Burrage, R. L., Pomerville A., & Gone, J. P. (2019). American Indian historical trauma: Anti-colonial prescriptions for healing, resilience, and survivance. *American Psychologist, 74*(1), 6–19. https://doi.org/10.1037/amp0000326

Hatfield, E., & Rapson, R. L. (2005). *Love and sex: Cross-cultural perspectives.* Lanham, MD: University Press of America.

Hauff, B. (2019, September 5). Man who murdered LGBTQ teen in Cortez is released from prison. *The Journal.* Retrieved from https://www.the-journal.com/articles/man-who-murdered-lgbtq-teen-in-cortez-is-released-from-prison/

Hays, P. A. (2022). *Addressing cultural complexities in counseling and clinical practice: An intersectional approach.* Washington, DC: American Psychological Association.

H.Con.Res. 331, 100th Cong., H. Rept 100–1031 (1988) (enacted).

Herdt, G. H. (Ed.). (1994). *Third sex, third gender: Beyond sexual dimorphism in culture and history.* New York, NY: Zone Books.

Innes, R. A., & Anderson, K. (Eds.). (2015). *Indigenous men and masculinities: Legacies, identities, regeneration.* Winnipeg, Manitoba, Canada: University of Manitoba Press.

Johns, M. M., Pingel, E., Eisenberg, A., Santana, M. L., & Bauermeister, J. (2012). Butch tops and femme bottoms? Sexual positioning, sexual decision making, and gender roles among young gay men. *American Journal of Men's Health, 6*(6), 505–518. https://doi.org/10.1177/1557988312455214

Johnson, D. (Ed.) (2018). *Diverse bodies, diverse practices: Toward an inclusive somatics.* Berkeley, CA: North Atlantic Books.

Jolivétte, A. (2016). *Indian blood: HIV and colonial trauma in San Francisco's Two-Spirit community.* Seattle, WA: University of Washington Press.

Katz, J. (1976). *Gay American history.* New York, NY: Thomas Y. Crowell.

Katz, J. N., Duggan, L., & Vidal, G. (1995). *The invention of heterosexuality.* New York, NY: Plume.

Krans, K. (2019). *Wild unknown archetypes deck and guidebook.* New York, NY: Harper Collins.

Kuhn, R. (2006). Two nations. On *Proof.* [CD]

Kuhn, R. (2013). Before I Rise. On *Live for the Light.* [Digital]

Kuhn, R. (2018). Fieldwork. In D. Johnson, (Ed.), *Diverse bodies, diverse practices: Toward an inclusive somatics.* Berkeley, CA: North Atlantic Books.

Kuhn, R. (2021, June). Somacultural Liberation [Speech]. University of Michigan Alumni Weekend. Online.

Levine, P. (2008). *Waking the tiger: Healing trauma.* Berkeley, CA: North Atlantic Books.

Lugar, S. (2013). Father figure: On dangerous daddies and cross-generational desire. *Studies in Gender and Sexuality, 14*(2), 153–157. https://doi.org/10.1080/15240657.2013.791603

Martin, B., & Dalzen, R. (2021). *The art of receiving and giving: The wheel of consent.* Eugene, OR: Luminare Press.

Martín-Baró, I., Aron A. (Ed.) & Corne, S. (Ed.). (1994). *Writings for a liberation psychology.* Cambridge, MA: Harvard University Press.

Mead, M. (1949). *Male and female: A study of the sexes in a changing world.* New York, NY: William Morrow.

Monkman, K. (2019, December 23). *Miss chief Eagle Testickle, Kent Monkman's alter ego.* The Metropolitan Museum of Art. https://www.metmuseum.org/perspectives/articles/2019/12/kent-monkman-miss-chief-eagle-testickle

Morgensen, S. (2015). Cutting to the roots of colonial masculinity. In K. Anderson & R. A. Innes (Eds.), *Indigenous men and masculinities: Legacies, identities, regeneration* (pp. 38–61). Winnipeg, Manitoba, Canada: University of Manitoba Press.

Morgensen, S. L. (2011). *Spaces between us: Queer settler colonialism and Indigenous decolonization.* Minneapolis, MN: University of Minnesota Press.

Moskowitz, D. A., Rieger, G., & Roloff, M. E. (2008). Tops, bottoms and versatiles. *Sexual and Relationship Therapy, 23*(3), 191–202. https://doi.org/10.1080/14681990802027259

Mowlabocus, S. (2010). *Gaydar culture: Gay men technology and embodiment in the digital age.* Farnham, UK: Ashgate.

Nakkach, S. (2003). "Bliss." On *Invocation* (CD).The Relaxation Company.

National Oceanic and Atmospheric Administration, Office for Coastal Management. (n.d.). American Indian Religious Freedom Act. Retrieved from https://coast.noaa.gov/data/Documents/OceanLawSearch/Summary%20of%20Law%20-%20American%20Indian%20Religious%20Freedom%20Act.pdf

Nibley, L. (Director) (2009). *Two Spirits.* Say Yes Quickly [Theater].

Noble, S. U. (2018). *Algorithms of oppression: How search engines enforce racism.* New York, NY: New York University Press.

Noelle, M. (2002). The ripple effect of the Matthew Shepard murder: Impact on the assumptive worlds of members of the targeted group. *American Behavioral Scientist, 46*(1), 27–50.

Ott, B., & Aoki, E. (2002). The politics of negotiating public tragedy: Media framing of the Matthew Shepard murder. *Rhetoric & Public Affairs, 5*(3), 483–505.

Oyeneyin, T. (2022). *Speak: Find your voice, trust your gut, and get from where you are to where you want to be.* New York, NY: Gallery Books.

Prenn, N. (2009). I second that emotion! On self- disclosure and its metaprocessing. In A. Bloomgarden & R. Mennuti (Eds.), *Psychotherapist revealed: Therapists speak about self-disclosure in psychotherapy* (pp. 85–99). New York, NY: Routledge/Taylor & Francis Group.

Prince-Hughes, T. (1998). Contemporary Two-Spirit identity in the fiction of Paula Gunn Allen and Beth Brant. *Studies in American Indian Literatures, 10*(4), 9–32.

Reay, B., Attwood, N., & Gooder, C. (2012) Inventing sex: The short history of sex addiction. *Sexuality and Culture, 17*(1), 1–19. https://doi.org/10.1007/s12119-012-9136-3

Rifkin, M. (2011a). The erotics of sovereignty. In Q.-L. Driskill, C. Finley, B. J. Gilley, & S. L. Morgensen (Eds.), *Queer Indigenous studies: Critical interventions in theory, politics, and literature* (pp. 172–189). Tucson, AZ: University of Arizona Press.

Rifkin, M. (2011b). *When did Indians become straight? Kinship, the history of sexuality, and Native sovereignty.* New York, NY: Oxford University Press.

Roscoe, W. (1987). Bibliography of berdache and alternative gender roles among North American Indians. *Journal of Homosexuality, 14*(3–4), 81–171. https://doi.org/10.1300/J082v14n03_06

Roscoe, W. (Ed.). (1988). *Living the spirit: A gay American Indian anthology.* New York, NY: St. Martin's Press.

Roscoe, W. (1991). *The Zuni man-woman.* Albuquerque, NM: University of New Mexico Press.

Roscoe, W. (1998). *Changing ones: Third and fourth genders in Native North America.* New York, NY: St. Martin's Griffin.

Ross, M. W. (2005). Typing, doing, and being: Sexuality and the internet. *Journal of Sex Research, 42*(4), 342–352. https://doi.org/10.1080/00224490509552290

Roth, G. (1997). *Sweat your prayers: Movement as spiritual practice.* New York, NY: Penguin Putnam.

S.227 - Savanna's Act. (2020, October 10). 116th Congress (2019–2020). https://www.congress.gov/bill/116th-congress/senate-bill/227

SAA. (2016). Our program of recovery from sex addiction. https://saa-recovery.org/our-program/

Sedgwick, E. K. (2008). *Epistemology of the closet.* Oakland, CA: University of California Press.

Siegel, D. J. (1999). *The developing mind: How relationships and the brain interact to shape who we are.* New York, NY: Guilford Press.

Simpson, L. B. (2017). *As we have always done.* Minneapolis, MN: University of Minnesota Press.

Smith, A. (2011). Queer theory and Native studies: The heteronormativity of settler colonialism. In Q.-L. Driskill, C. Finley, B. J. Gilley, & S. L. Morgensen (Eds.), *Queer Indigenous studies: Critical interventions in theory, politics, and literature* (pp. 43–65). Tucson, AZ: University of Arizona Press.

Smith, L. T. (1999). *Decolonizing methodologies: Research and indigenous peoples.* London, UK: Zed Books.

Sovereign Bodies Institute. (n.d.). Retrieved March 18, 2023, from https://www.sovereign-bodies.org/

Stolorow, R. D., Brandchaft, B., & Atwood, G. E., (1987). *Psychoanalytic treatment: An intersubjective approach.* Hillsdale, NJ: The Analytic Press.

Takacs, D. (2003). How does your positionality bias your epistemology? *Thought & Action, 27*, 27–38. Retrieved from http://repository.uchastings.edu/faculty_scholarship/1264

Tatonetti, L. (2014). *The queerness of Native American literature.* Minneapolis, MN: University of Minnesota Press.

Taylor, S. R. (2018). *The body is not an apology: The power of radical self-love.* Oakland, CA: Berrett-Koehler.

Trask, H. K. (2004). The color of violence. *Social Justice, 31*(4), 8–16.

Trexler, R. C. (1997). *Sex and conquest: Gendered violence, political order, and the European conquest of the Americas.* Ithaca, NY: Cornell University Press.

Trexler, R. C. (2002). Making the American berdache: Choice or constraint? *Journal of Social History, 35*(3), 613–636. https://doi.org/10.1353/jsh.2002.0033

Tuck, E., & Yang, K. W. (2012). Decolonization is not a metaphor. *Decolonization: Indigeneity, Education & Society, 1*(1), 1–40.

Two-Spirited People of Manitoba Inc. (2019). We belong. Accessed December 2019. Retrieved from https://twospiritmanitoba.ca/

US Department of the Interior, Office of the Secretary Office of the Assistant Secretary—Indian Affairs. (2014). *2013 American Indian population and labor force report.* Retrieved from https://www.bia.gov/sites/bia.gov/files/assets/public/pdf/idc1-024782.pdf

US States Department of Justice (n.d.) *Matthew Shepard & James Byrd, Jr., Hate Crimes Prevention Act of 2009.* Retrieved from http://www.justice.gov/crt/about/crm/matthewshepard.php

Vernon, I. S. (2001). *Killing us quietly: Native Americans and HIV/AIDS.* Lincoln, NE: University of Nebraska Press.

Vizenor, G. (Ed.). (2008). *Survivance: Narratives of Native presence.* Lincoln, NE: University of Nebraska Press.

Watkins, M., & Shulman, H. (2010). *Toward psychologies of liberation*. Houndmills, UK: Palgrave Macmillan.

Williams, W. L. (1986). *The spirit and the flesh: Sexual diversity in American Indian culture.* Boston, MA: Beacon Press.

Wilson, W. A., & Yellow Bird, M. (Eds.). (2005). *For Indigenous eyes only: A decolonization handbook.* Santa Fe, NM: School of American Research Press.

Wilson, W. A., & Yellow Bird, M. (Eds.). (2012). *For Indigenous minds only: A decolonization handbook.* Santa Fe, NM: School for Advanced Research Press.

INDEX

A

D

N

O

P

S

U

V

W

Z

ABOUT THE AUTHOR

Roger Kuhn, PhD, is a Poarch Creek Two-Spirit Indigiqueer somacultural activist, artist, sex therapist, and sexuality educator. Roger's work explores the concepts of decolonizing and unsettling sexuality and focuses on the way culture impacts and informs our bodily experiences. In addition to his work as a licensed psychotherapist, he is a board member of the American Indian Cultural Center of San Francisco, a board member and community organizer of the Bay Area American Indian Two-Spirits Powwow, a board member of the American Association of Sexuality Educators, Counselors and Therapists, and a member of the LGBTQI+ Advisory Committee of the San Francisco Human Rights Commission. In 2022, Roger was featured in the Levi's Pride campaign. His writing appears in publications from North Atlantic Books, Anthem Press, and *Yellow Medicine Review*. He has released five independent music albums. Kuhn lives in Guerneville, California.

ABOUT
NORTH ATLANTIC BOOKS

North Atlantic Books (NAB) is an independent, nonprofit publisher committed to a bold exploration of the relationships between mind, body, spirit, and nature. Founded in 1974, NAB aims to nurture a holistic view of the arts, sciences, humanities, and healing. To make a donation or to learn more about our books, authors, events, and newsletter, please visit www.northatlanticbooks.com.